CAN PEOPLE LEARN TO LEARN?

How to Know Each Other

WORLD PERSPECTIVES

Volumes already published

WORLD PERSPECTIVES • *Volume Eighteen*

Planned and Edited by RUTH NANDA ANSHEN

CAN PEOPLE LEARN TO LEARN?

How to Know Each Other

George

BY BROCK CHISHOLM

New York

HARPER & BROTHERS PUBLISHERS

Library of Congress catalog card number: 56–11072

Contents

World Perspectives

What This Series Means

IT IS the thesis of *World Perspectives* that man is in the process of developing a new consciousness which, in spite of his apparent spiritual and moral captivity, can eventually lift the human race above and beyond the fear, ignorance, brutality and isolation which beset it today. It is to this nascent consciousness, to this concept of man born out of a universe perceived through a fresh vision of reality, that *World Perspectives* is dedicated.

Only those spiritual and intellectual leaders of our epoch who have a paternity in this extension of man's horizons are invited to participate in this Series: those who are aware of the truth that beyond the divisiveness among men there exists a primordial unitive power since we are all bound together by a common humanity more fundamental than any unity of dogma; those who recognize that the centrifugal force which has scattered and atomized mankind must be replaced by an integrating structure and process capable of bestowing meaning and purpose on existence; those who realize that science itself, when not inhibited by the limitations of its own methodology, when chastened and humbled, commits man to an indeterminate range of yet undreamed consequences that may flow from it.

This Series endeavors to point to a reality of which scientific theory has revealed only one aspect. It is the commitment to this reality that lends universal intent to a scientist's most original and solitary thought. By acknowledging this frankly we shall restore science to the great family of human aspirations by which men hope to fulfill themselves in the world community as thinking and sentient beings. For our problem is to discover a principle of differentiation and yet relationship lucid enough to justify and to purify scientific, philosophic and all other knowledge, both discursive and intuitive, by accepting their interdependence. This is the crisis in consciousness made articulate through the crisis in science. This is the new awakening.

Each volume presents the thought and belief of its author and points to the way in which religion, philosophy, art, science, economics, politics and history may constitute that form of human activity which takes the fullest and most precise account of variousness, possibility, complexity and difficulty. Thus *World Perspectives* endeavors to define that ecumenical power of the mind and heart which enables man through his mysterious greatness to re-create his life.

This Series is committed to a re-examination of all those sides of human endeavor which the specialist was taught to believe he could safely leave aside. It interprets present and past events impinging on human life in our growing World Age and envisages what man may yet attain when summoned by an unbending inner necessity to the quest of what is most exalted in him. Its purpose is to offer new vistas in terms of world and human development while refusing to betray the intimate correlation between universality and individuality, dynamics and form, freedom and destiny. Each author deals with the increasing realization that spirit and nature are not separate and apart; that intuition and reason must regain their importance as the means of perceiving and fusing inner being with outer reality.

World Perspectives endeavors to show that the conception of wholeness, unity, organism is a higher and more concrete conception than that of matter and energy. Thus an enlarged meaning of life, of biology, not as it is revealed in the test tube of the laboratory but as it is experienced within the organism of life itself, is attempted in this Series. For the principle of life consists in the tension which connects spirit with the realm of matter. The element of life is dominant in the very texture of nature, thus rendering life, biology, a trans-empirical science. The laws of life have their origin beyond their mere physical manifestations and compel us to consider their spiritual source. In fact, the widening of the conceptual framework has not only served to restore order within the respective branches of knowledge, but has also disclosed analogies in man's position regarding the analysis and synthesis of experience in apparently separated domains of knowledge suggesting the possibility of an ever more embracing objective description of the meaning of life.

Knowledge, it is shown in these books, no longer consists in a manipulation of man and nature as opposite forces, nor in the reduction of data to mere statistical order, but is a means of liberating mankind from the destructive power of fear, pointing the way toward the goal of the rehabilitation of the human will and the rebirth of faith and confidence in the human person. The works published also endeavor to reveal that the cry for patterns, systems and authorities is growing less insistent as the desire grows stronger in both East and West for the recovery of a dignity, integrity and self-realization which are the inalienable rights of man who may now guide change by means of conscious purpose in the light of rational experience.

Other vital questions explored relate to problems of international understanding as well as to problems dealing with prejudice and the resultant tensions and antagonisms. The growing perception and responsibility of our World Age point to the new reality that the individual person and the collective person supplement and integrate each other; that the thrall of totalitarianism of both left and right has been shaken in the universal desire to recapture the authority of truth and human totality. Mankind can finally place its trust not in a proletarian authoritarianism, not in a secularized humanism, both of which have betrayed the spiritual property right of history, but in a sacramental brotherhood and in the unity of knowledge. This new consciousness has created a widening of human horizons beyond every parochialism, and a revolution in human thought comparable to the basic assumption, among the ancient Greeks, of the sovereignty of reason; corresponding to the great effulgence of the moral conscience articulated by the Hebrew prophets; analogous to the fundamental assertions of Christianity; or to the beginning of a new scientific era, the era of the science of dynamics, the experimental foundations of which were laid by Galileo in the Renaissance.

An important effort of this Series is to re-examine the contradictory meanings and applications which are given today to such terms as democracy, freedom, justice, love, peace, brotherhood and God. The purpose of such inquiries is to clear the way for the foundation of a genuine *world* history not in terms of nation or race or culture but in terms of man in relation to God, to himself, his fellow man and the universe, that reach beyond immediate self-interest. For the meaning of the World Age consists in respecting man's hopes and dreams which lead to a deeper understanding of the basic values of all peoples.

World Perspectives is planned to gain insight into the meaning of man, who not only is determined by history but who also determines history. History is to be understood as concerned not only with the life of man on this planet but as including also such cosmic influences as interpenetrate our human world. This generation is discovering that history does not conform to the social optimism of modern civilization and that the organization of human communities and the establishment of freedom and peace are not only intellectual achievements but spiritual and moral achievements as well, demanding a cherishing of the wholeness of human personality, the "unmediated wholeness of feeling and thought," and constituting a never-ending challenge to man, emerging from the abyss of meaninglessness and suffering, to be renewed and replenished in the totality of his life.

Justice itself, which has been "in a state of pilgrimage and crucifixion" and now is being slowly liberated from the grip of social and political demonologies in the East as well as in the West, begins to question its own premises. The modern revolutionary movements which have challenged the sacred institutions of society by protecting social injustice in the name of social justice are examined and re-evaluated.

In the light of this, we have no choice but to admit that the *un*-freedom against which freedom is measured must be retained with it, namely, that the aspect of truth out of which the night view appears to emerge, the darkness of our time, is as little abandonable as is man's subjective advance. Thus the two sources of man's consciousness are inseparable, not as dead but as living and complementary, an aspect of that "principle of complementarity" through which Niels Bohr has sought to unite the quantum and the wave, both of which constitute the very fabric of life's radiant energy.

There is in mankind today a counterforce to the sterility and danger of a quantitative, anonymous mass culture, a new, if sometimes, imperceptible, spiritual sense of convergence toward world unity on the basis of the sacredness of each human person and respect for the plurality of cultures. There is a growing awareness that equality may not be evaluated in mere numerical terms but is proportionate and analogical in its reality. For when equality is equated with interchangeability, individuality is negated and the human person extinguished.

We stand at the brink of an age of the world in which human life presses forward to actualize new forms. The false separation of man and nature, of time and space, of freedom and security, is acknowledged and we are faced with a new vision of man in his organic unity and of history offering a richness and diversity of quality and majesty of scope hitherto unprecedented. In relating the accumulated wisdom of man's spirit to the new reality of the World Age, in articulating its thought and belief, *World Perspectives* seeks to encourage a renaissance of hope in society and of pride in man's decision as to what his destiny will be.

World Perspectives is committed to the recognition that all great changes are preceded by a vigorous intellectual re-evaluation and reorganization. Our authors are aware that the sin of hubris may be avoided by showing that the creative process itself is not a free activity if by free we mean arbitrary, or unrelated to cosmic law. For the creative process in the human mind, the developmental processes in organic nature and the basic laws of the inorganic realm may be but varied expressions of a universal formative process. Thus *World Perspectives* hopes to show that although the present apocalyptic period is one of exceptional tensions, there is also at work an exceptional movement toward a compensating unity which refuses to violate the ultimate moral power at work in the universe, that very power upon which all human effort must at last depend. In this way we may come to understand that there exists an inherent independence of spiritual and mental growth which though conditioned by circumstances is never determined by circumstances. In this way the great plethora of human knowledge may be correlated with an insight into the nature of human nature by being attuned to the wide and deep range of human thought and human experience.

In spite of the infinite obligation of men and in spite of their finite power, in spite of the intransigence of nationalisms, and in spite of the homelessness of moral passions rendered ineffectual by the scientific outlook, beneath the apparent turmoil and upheaval of the present, and out of the transformations of this dynamic period with the unfolding of a world consciousness, the purpose of *World Perspectives* is to help quicken the "unshaken heart of well-rounded truth" and interpret the significant elements of the World Age now taking shape out of the core of that undimmed continuity of the creative process which restores man to mankind while deepening and enhancing his communion with the universe.

RUTH NANDA ANSHEN

New York, 1958

CAN PEOPLE LEARN TO LEARN?

How to Know Each Other

I.

Prologue

EVER since anything has been known of man's social development, group welfare has apparently been a matter of great concern to those of each community best able to think and act effectively. However, that concern has usually been limited to the welfare of some relatively small group. Throughout the earlier history of developing man, the family, or an enlarged family, the tribe, was both the social unit and the area to which social responsibility was limited.

During the earlier centuries each family, or tribe, was almost entirely self-contained, depending on outsiders for little if anything. Wherever something was in short supply and not locally available, women, cattle, food or slaves, commonly the shortages were made good by raids or invasion and occupation of the land of other tribes. Normally no concern was felt for the welfare of outsiders, and still much of that ancient, and anachronistic, limitation of feelings of responsibility is to be found throughout the world. Of course the definition of the area of responsibility has changed in most places. At this or that time or place it has become less familial or tribal and more a matter of geographic, racial, color, class, economic, religious, national or some other such expanded, but still limiting, concept.

During the long period of relatively little communication across physical barriers such as mountains, deserts or oceans, and when commercial contacts were episodic and unorganized raiding or trading expeditions, the development of any community of interest beyond the tribe, or later principality or city-state, was, of course, very slow. Gradually, however, certain progressive individuals began to discover that, for their own commercial advantage, they needed to establish permanent relationships with trustworthy persons in other places, other cities, other countries. Through such relationships between mutually trusted individuals, and to the advantage of both, it became possible to establish credits, bills of exchange, and eventually very complicated systems of exchange of goods and services.

Many such commercial arrangements functioned quite independently of political relationships and often survived political upheavals. These arrangements gradually developed a network of mutually responsible individuals and commercial and banking houses, and with that development some degree of concern for the welfare of at least certain persons outside the local community. That concern did not infect the political or the general population until much later and has still far to go before it becomes universal.

Even yet for most people in all countries their own food supply, tax rate, local politics, sports, prestige and feelings of power, competitive standard of living or many other minor values are given more consideration than the welfare, even the survival, of the human race. It may be that the world problems are too complex, too big, too unapproachable for the "man in the street" to try to think about without producing an almost intolerable feeling of frustration and futility.

But it seems that a major reason for this persisting lack of concern for the welfare of others than one's own group is the early learning in homes of the traditional self- or group-centered attitudes of the parents. It is early in life that "consciences" acquire most of their values and criteria, and largely from parents. If father's most obvious concern is baseball, football, hockey, golf, fishing, horse or dog races, his political party, or the success of his own business, and mother's is her own clothes, social status, church group, the saving of her own soul, bridge or canasta or other club, or gossip about her friends, the child learns that these are the right and proper areas for the focusing of adult attention. These points of view and scales of values are being established in the developing personality of the child, and his conscience will include no feelings of obligation in relation to any values not illustrated by his parents.

If parents are ardent partisans of their union, their club, their church, their social or color or racial or economic or national group, and against all other competing groups, their children will probably develop loyalties to values outside their own pleasures or comfort, but those loyalties will always tend to be limited to narrow groups with which a close identification is felt. Differences will be felt to be threatening and only conformity acceptable and safe.

Yet it seems evident that world problems do need to be thought about, and very seriously, if we are to have reasonable hope of survival of our race. It is true that a direct attack at a world level by any individual on the major world problems, food shortages, population increase, "cold war," armaments, atomic energy, rigid faiths, nationalism, racial discrimination, aggression (our own and other people's), imperialism (colonial or commercial), and many others, is hopeless, and can lead only to defeat. It does not follow, however, that nothing can be done about all these and other pressing dangers, nor does it follow that they must or can be left to "leaders," politicians or experts. Leaders (as distinct from dictators) will or can lead, eventually, only where their people want to go; politicians almost invariably follow far behind the more constructive thinkers among the people, and experts are commonly far too narrow in their experience and concept, and in any case cannot do the job alone. Dictators are, most of the time, too busy locally, maintaining their precarious positions, to deal constructively with world problems.

If these dangers to our race are to be dealt with effectively, it is we, the ordinary people of the world, who will have to assume the burden of trying to understand them, and we might well concern ourselves first with the question of approach. When trying to see a large problem objectively, it is often useful to try to break it down into categories, or parts of a manageable size, so that a clearer picture may be seen of just what the problem really involves, what the basic and contributing causes are, what experiments or changes might be desirable, whether such changes are barred by firmly held faiths, prejudices, loyalties, taboos, customs or vested interests, and whether and how the job to be done can be spread among many people.

It may also be useful to search for important common factors among the causes or conditions of these dangers. If there are such factors, progress toward solution of one problem may contribute greatly to the solution of others. Such attempts to see problems clearly may suggest areas of responsibility—who might do what toward their solution—and also perhaps some indication of any necessary stages in progress toward solutions may be found.

Of course some of these problems have been examined extensively and repeatedly. For example the Population Commission of the Economic and Social Council of the United Nations has examined the facts about world population, but it has confined its considerations to mere description. It has drawn a true and terrifying picture of the calamitous rate of increase in numbers of people in the world but is very shy of offering recommendations toward solutions. Its terms of reference include the responsibility of making such recommendations to the Economic and Social Council, and through that body to the United Nations General Assembly, but a widespread taboo and organized resistance on the part of one religious sect has prevented any constructive results.

Others of these problems have been studied but apparently almost always from the point of view of some local or group values, or under the control of limiting original premises or some loyalty or taboo. It is not easy for any of us to see clearly and truly anything which lies in areas in relation to which our culture or subculture takes firm attitudes. These cultural or group certainties, taboos, faiths, or anxieties, color and distort our observations without our recognition, and perhaps our main problem in attempting any study is to see through the shadows thrown by our own prejudices about what is "right" or "proper" or "good" or "safe" or "moral" or "democratic" or "Christian" or some other classification of possible answers. It is clearly impossible too for any of us to look at world problems from all points of view, that is, from the points of view of all kinds of people in the world. A Norwegian fisherman, a Chinese laborer, an American bond dealer, a South African native miner, a Swiss watchmaker, a Korean farmer, a French artist, a Russian engineer, and everyone else everywhere, all are vitally affected by such problems as are suggested above, and valid solutions must eventually prove useful and acceptable for all kinds of people everywhere, though of course people's attitudes, and what is acceptable to them, may change.

Many studies will have to be made before a clear picture of all the conditions affecting these problems can be seen. At this time our tentative approach must inevitably be sketchy, but our main concern should be to keep it universal, attempting to avoid our own cultural prejudices, whatever and wherever our culture.

We might well try to use our imagination in one of its major roles, that of exploration of new ground without commitment or penalty, though we may find that our particular training has to some extent crippled that very valuable faculty. In order to discount or to try to discount the accident of our own culture, it might be helpful to imagine ourselves visitors from some other planet, Mars perhaps, but without the warlike attitudes ancient myth and present astrology would ascribe to that planet. We might try to imagine ourselves free of the history of the place where we have happened to live, free of all preconceptions as to rights and wrongs, free of all certainties imposed on us when we were children, free of all loyalties to particular accidental and temporal patterns of living among which we happened to be brought up, but concerned only with the welfare of all individuals of the human race.

Let us try to put ourselves in the place and conditions of living of various people, attempting to feel with them some of their preoccupations and to see world problems from their point of view. We may start anywhere, spin a globe, point a finger, and imagine:

II.

The Nations

WE, THE people of a group of nations, are caught between centuries. Some of us want to keep the best of two worlds, but often the best for ourselves, not necessarily the best for our people. We have long been educated in disregard for cause-and-effect relationships. Our religion has been largely responsible for that type of education, or rather the use made of our religion by power-hungry politicians.

Politically most of us have gained complete independence, but this is a new situation, not known in many of our countries for generations. We have felt justified for so long in being against governmental authority that it is hard for us to become responsible and constructive. Our political instruments are still far too often rabble rousing and civil riot, assassination and *coup d'état*. In our political discussions invective, name calling and character assassination are still usual, but we are learning from our own mistakes as we never could when under the tutelage of foreign armies and administrators.

The required acceptance and obedience, the submission to "Kismet," one's fate, the prescribed praying and eating rituals and almsgiving, common to the many millions of adherents of our religion, have stressed and largely kept intact the unity of our peoples under the one universal God. True we are now split into many sects, but basically we are all one in relation to God and His Prophet.

It may be that the certainty of Paradise for the faithful has minimized the importance of other values for our people, and has allowed the continuance of social conditions quite inappropriate for countries with our long history of science and learning. Recently, however, we

6

are changing and some of us hope that when we have been able to raise the level of the health and the standard of living of our people, we may then soon develop above the level of our present stage of acute nationalism.

One very sharp thorn in our side, felt by almost all of us to be an aggression and an insult, is the taking over of part of our lands by descendants of the very people who first stood out against the spread of our faith. Though we have always honored, even adopted, their God, and also their prophets, they would have none of ours and have always remained segregated. Now, with the help of great nations, they have taken our land, evicted our people, and fought fanatically for their foothold, and with the apparent intention of enlarging it. We are firmly resolved to resist, and hope that over a period of years, perhaps many years, the financial support they receive from their coreligionists all over the world will diminish and their economy, isolated locally by our steadfast intention, will not be able to survive. We will never accept, and we do not want, their technical help in our economic development, though some few of us recognize how valuable it could be if we could use it.

In the meantime the million or so refugees from their aggression are a heavy charge on our resources, though helped a little by United Nations assistance.

We honestly cannot understand the appeal to justice on the part of these aggressors or its support by nations otherwise friendly to us. To our minds there is a far better case for giving America, or at least a few of the states, back to the Indians than for our surrendering territory we have owned for many centuries.

Of one thing we are sure; we must be stronger than we have ever been since the days of our great expansion. We were shocked that we were not able to push the invaders into the sea, and some of us recognize that our own lack of ability to trust and co-operate with each other, to sink our special interests in the service of a common cause, was, and is, a major source of our weakness.

We begin to recognize that our people themselves are not healthy enough, physically, mentally or socially, to compete effectively in the world as it is now. Trachoma, bilharziasis, tuberculosis, malaria, yaws and many other diseases must be brought under control. More and better food must be produced and better distributed. We must develop our own industries and not continue to depend on other people for so much of what we need. We all look with hope and high expectation to the United Nations for the kinds of help we need, but most of us would like to keep clear of lesser alliances which would align us against the special political and economic interests of other groups, a position we have found in the past to be dangerous. In several of our countries violent social revolutions are taking place. After some years during which we profited very little from the exploitation of our oil resources by foreigners, we have forced them to give us a more reasonable share of their vast earnings. Some of us had believed that we ourselves could take over the development of our own resources, but we have found that our people are not ready for that degree of responsibility. Much technical training, but also much social development, will be needed before we can handle such major operations successfully, but the recently proven ability of one of our governments to operate the Suez Canal has encouraged us greatly.

Individual responsibility is still rare among our peoples. Our education has been too narrow, too local, too much controlled by religion, and too much confined to the upper social classes, who have usually concerned themselves only for their own profit or power.

Very few of our people will willingly perform a full day's work regularly every day. This is not just "laziness"; tradition, climate, chronic diseases, malnutrition, fatalism resting on the doctrine of predestination, and the fact that in our culture hard work has rarely if ever brought fortune, all play a part in our reluctance to work at a pressure that would enable us to compete with the highly productive nations.

On the other hand, our religion has always encouraged aggression, particularly against infidels who resist conversion, and has promised immediate entry to Paradise for soldiers killed in a war officially designated a "Holy War."

The slowness of our culture to adapt itself to the modern world may be ascribed, at least in large part, to the fact that we have a rigid and final authority in the Koran and the Sunna. That authority deals with practically all aspects of life. Most of us insist that, unlike the Christian Bible, it is a consistent whole and far more precise in its instructions to the faithful, but some of us begin to see that, like the Bible, it makes no provision for the world changes which could not be foreseen by the prophet, and there are really many inconsistencies. As with all written constitutions, its effect is to make changes, even very necessary changes, unduly difficult and often to delay them tragically. All our cultures for centuries have shown great contrast between utter misery and poverty among most of our people on the one hand, and on the other, for a few of our people, great luxury and wealth. Reform in our land-tenure systems is one of the crying needs of our whole region. It has been begun in some of our countries but there is still a very long way to go.

Canada

We, the people of a nation, are well fed, prosperous and self-satisfied. We are somewhat inclined to criticize the attitudes and behavior of other less fortunate people, and imply that they should follow our pattern to gain prosperity, wealth and stability. When, or if, we stop to think, we know that is not true. We are simply the fortunate inheritors, from aggressive ancestors, of vast land and water areas, and enormous reserves of natural resources, and we have been able to develop a stable form of government. That form of government suits our people, and allows us to get on with our economic and social development with a minimum of fuss and digression, and as rapidly as the prejudices and divisions of our people will allow.

We are a divided people in a vast and divided country; great mountain and forest barriers as well as economic, climatic, cultural, language and religious differences separate us into groups with many conflicting attitudes and interests.

We have kept close contact with our European origins and, though politically entirely independent, we form part of a great commonwealth of nations and share a common monarchy with most of its members. The monarchy is very dear to us, providing the symbol and focus for our sentiment and for our sense of continuity and of belonging in the fellowship of the commonwealth, though we are also distinctly American in many of our attitudes, methods and institutions.

Some of us are greatly concerned about many of the influences threatening to infiltrate us across our southern border. We are almost unanimous in disliking secret police, loyalty oaths and investigations, irresponsible politicians, the screaming advertising and adulation of movie and television stars and even of politicians that choke our radio and television channels, and we hope that someday our great and beloved neighbor will moderate these and some other of the objectionable features of a culture whose constructive aspects we admire so much and seek to emulate.

Some of our feelings may well be the result of the quite human and natural jealousy of a relatively small population for a large and powerful one; some of them may perhaps arise from resentment of a certain patronizing attitude we sometimes think we see across the border. These feelings, however, are far outweighed by our very real appreciation of the unique degree of tolerance of our independences, and even defiances, that our great neighbor has shown for many years. It is long since we have felt that we had any need to maintain defenses along our southern border. That is very fortunate for us, as our border is not defensible even by several times our small population, and we are grateful for a degree of forbearance shown by few great nations.

About one third of our total population is French-speaking, but most of us of that group do not speak modern French but our own dialect, which has not changed with the French of the outside world. We use many old words and forms not known now in France. We are the descendants of the first Europeans to colonize northern North America, and this has been our homeland for many generations.

We hold fast to many of our ancient customs. Our provincial law, because we are concentrated mostly in one province, is founded on Napoleonic not English law. Women still have relatively few rights in our provinces, and we have instituted compulsory education for everyone only recently. Our educational system has been developed by, and largely for the purposes of, the priesthood, and higher education for our women is still not usual.

For many of us, particularly in rural areas, social patterns, normal and acceptable in other countries, and even among our own coreligionists, are declared "mortal sin" by our priests. We are forbidden to marry outside our own church. In the army during the war many of us were forbidden, on the threat of hell-fire, to learn English. We have been kept poor by the excessive share of our earnings which must go to the already wealthy church, and we have been kept ignorant by a provincial educational system, and in other provinces by separate schools, which are primarily religious, which make all living subservient to the church.

Our priests and politicians, combined in their need to keep us apart from the rest of our country, have always told us that we are taken advantage of and exploited by the English-speaking people. We have been taught to fight against those other people, never to co-operate with them except to our advantage. The old hate of the conquered for the conquerors has been stimulated and kept alive to serve the special interests of the politicians and of the priests.

Only very gradually, and fearfully, are we beginning to rebel against this domination of our behavior and of our very thinking. We have been so frightened in childhood of the power the church has assumed, both here and for eternity, that to free ourselves of that domination is a very slow and bitter struggle. Still only a few of us dare raise our voices against our masters, but the numbers are growing. Most of us are too deeply committed, too used to living under the control of the church, its threats of eternal punishment, and its protection and assurances of reward for obedience in a future life, too impressed with its political and social power, to dare to risk the threat of ostracism, excommunication and loss of employment which always hangs over us. We have all our lives been obedient and left all the thinking to the priests; it is impossible for most of us to begin to think for ourselves now.

Some of us, hating our servitude but not able to think for ourselves or live free of controls, believe that communism is our best answer. It is much easier to escape from one orthodoxy to another than to learn to think for ourselves, and communism offers rewards of power and control of others in this world, not in a life after death. Some of us recognize the fact that the methods of control, of both behavior and thought, are almost identical in the two systems.

The transition is not difficult, and some of us see no other convictions strong enough to compete with the absolutes with which we have always lived.

Both systems would harness us to their own need for power, both promise us rich rewards in the future, but both deprive us of the great right of freedom of man to think for himself and take responsibility for his own decisions. We have never known that freedom, but more and more of us begin to see that it does exist for some people. We, too, could be free to grow if we could break through the control of our consciences, but our consciences were strongly built in childhood and reinforced by very potent fear.

Some of us begin to see that it is not the English-speaking people who have exploited us and kept us poor, but our own religious and political masters. Of course, those masters, politicians and priests, have had the same early education that we have had, and they also have never learned to think freely and in terms of cause and effect. Inevitably, the short-term goals of their own powers and affluence, and the long-term goal of the wealth, glory and power of the church, appear to them to be valid, but time is on our side and the rising tide of our resolve to free ourselves is gaining strength.

Those of us who are English-speaking, descendants of ancestors of many countries, and including most of the million and a half immigrants of the last ten years, have stood aside from the very real problem of our French-speaking compatriots. We have been very busy with our own affairs, developing our industries, expanding our exports, establishing our country as a nation among the nations, and making much money for ourselves. We have shamefully neglected to learn the language of our French-speaking citizens. Without really knowing them and their peculiar problems, we have criticized them as backward, prejudiced and intolerant, while we ourselves well illustrate at least the last two of these same vices. We have been very complacent in our prosperity. True, we distribute something in charity through the United Nations and its specialized agencies, and through the Colombo Plan of the British Commonwealth, but not enough to hurt us or at all to threaten our own very high standard of living.

Since early in our history we have had to compromise between opposing interests. We have developed the habit of taking the middle course between European and American cultures, between Protestant and Roman Catholic pressures (we are distributed roughly equally between those two religious groups), between the English and French languages, and between the conflicting needs of the geographic, climatic, economic and political divisions of our country.

In international relationships we are also inclined to compromise, tending to take long-term attitudes, not supporting the more violent maneuvers of our friends, and seeking to exploit and develop agreement rather than to fight disagreements. Our political system allows our representatives at international meetings an amount of latitude and freedom to negotiate which is rare among the nations, and it is always possible for those representatives to consult directly with a dependable authority in our capital and quickly obtain a commitment from the government on any pressing matter which demands a firm statement of policy. That adjustability to changing circumstances is an enormous asset in negotiating with other countries. No one, and particularly our own representatives, ambassadors or delegates, need long remain in doubt as to what our government's policy is on any question. Our friends, and antagonists, know where we stand, and so regard us as reliable even when we are opposed to their wishes.

Our strength lies in our vast reserves of natural resources, our abundant space and our ability to produce both food and manufactured products, and our relatively high degree of political maturity. Our weakness lies in our internal divisions with far too little mutual understanding and mutual co-operation. Our English-speaking people should learn to speak French and to know and to co-operate with our French-speaking people, who on their part should free themselves from the outgrown controls they have inherited, learn to speak English and to co-operate with the rest of our population.

China

We, the people of a nation, over six hundred million of us, are full of enthusiasm and hope. For centuries our eyes were turned backward to our ancestors but recently, and painfully, we are learning to look at the present and future. We are no longer passive but feel like a giant waking from a long spell or illness. We will do big things, and probably make big mistakes.

Many of us do not like everything that is going on in our country, but our leaders are strong and are doing wonderful things for our people. For the first time in our long history we have real hope that the people themselves will benefit from the great changes being made from our ancient ways.

The cost has been and is heavy. Many have lost their lives because they did not welcome these changes, but we are used to much greater loss of life, in famines, in warfare, in pestilences, and our tendency is to accept what comes and make the best of it.

Hunger is still our greatest internal enemy. Unpredictable weather over large areas has always plagued us with drought and floods, and costs us millions of lives. Only a far more complete transportation and distribution system, extensive dams, irrigation and power plants, and mechanization of industry can support our vast and rapidly increasing population.

Foreigners and warlords have ravaged and exploited us for many centuries, but now we are feeling again our ancient strength and will increase that strength until it must be recognized by the whole world.

"Face," prestige, high regard, are major values for us and we cannot tolerate being kept out of the councils of the nations of the world, but we can make them fear us. Our vast manpower, our ruthlessness, our ability to work hard and live on very little, our developing industries, are already recognized as threats to the complacency of those who would keep us down.

We think that those who decry our methods have never experienced our problems. Most of them became prosperous by exploitation of land and natural resources which they took from weaker or less aggressive people or by economic imperialism, buying raw materials cheaply from less developed peoples and selling finished products dearly to those same people, and keeping markets open by force. Those methods of development have been closed to us because we have never, in the past, been aggressive people. We have always admired the intellectual and despised the soldier. Now we have had to learn from our conquerors that only from strength can negotiation and competition be successful. While they have been exploiting us by their methods of ruthless economic competition backed by force, they have sent us many missionaries to teach us the virtues of forbearance, meekness, peace and brotherly love, our own ancient virtues, but they have added miracles, magics and rituals, appropriate to a stage of development beyond which our thinking people had passed long ago.

At last we have recognized that all these recent importations would only continue and intensify our exploitation and dependence. Why should we tamely accept and practice ethical and social concepts which our teachers themselves have never allowed to restrain their own ruthless business methods? We are not alone in this rise against those who have used us for so long. We have a strong friend who appears to many of us a champion of freedom, though to many others of us a possible worse exploiter than those we have known in the past. Also all our cousins of this vast and heavily populated part of the world feel the same stirrings we do and are showing the same determination to live their own lives in their own ways. It is clear to us that meekness and forbearance will not save us from famine, starvation, graft and the corruption of our people. We have learned that we must ourselves be strong in the guns and airplanes and soldiers and whatever advanced methods of killing the western peoples use and will respect, for instance, napalm, gas, biologicals, or atomic weapons.

Some of us hope that some day we may all be able to trust ourselves and other nations not to try to exploit one another, but for a long time a world police force will surely be necessary. Some of us think that only through the United Nations can that, and peace, be attained, but many others feel that we can trust only our own kinds of people, and have hoped that the alliance with which we work now may attain and maintain a sufficiently stable control. Unless we and our friends are able to get what we consider fair consideration in the United Nations, the most aggressive of our leaders will continue to gain prestige.

In any case there will be no going back to our graft-ridden, factional, unstable and corrupt past. The symbol of that past still persists on an island off our shores and, backed by Western power, threatens us with invasion. We are determined that that intolerable situation shall not continue to lose us face, though we are not yet prepared to wage a full-scale war for survival.

Now we are very busy consolidating our social gains, both internally and externally. Our greatest handicap is the shortage of technically trained and experienced men and women, but we are doing all we can to establish adequate training facilities for all kinds of scientists and technicians. Already we are recognized widely as one of the greatest, if not the greatest, of leaders against colonialism. Now we must organize and develop internally so that our economic position also may become adequate for one of the world's leading nations. We have every expectation of filling that role, and soon.

In recent years, with better health services, better organized production and distribution of food, and beginning of flood control, our population increases at a frightening rate. Our government, aware of this great danger to our strength, has legitimized surgical abortion and many thousands of such operations are being performed. Still our numbers increase much too fast for our developing economy. As do so many other countries, we urgently need a method of preventing conception by some safe and efficient chemical or other means.

France

We, the people of a nation, are confused and bewildered. We have been a proud nation, but many of us begin to feel that something is wrong, not only with the world around us, that is evident, but with ourselves also.

We cannot seem to make our form of democracy work effectively. For years we have not had a government strong enough to reform our tax system, or even to collect our taxes. Our politicians seem to many of us to concern themselves more with personal prestige and power, personal antagonisms or attachments, and local interests than with the welfare of our country and our people as a whole. We find plenty of intelligent and devoted people among us, but their devotion is usually to some less than national, much less than world, good. They labor for a party, for an economic or ideological or religious group, or for the growers of sugar beets or of grapes.

They seem to take the strange attitude that a part is more important than the whole.

Many explanations have been offered. It has been suggested that our trouble is biological, that because such large numbers of our best young men have been killed, captured or crippled in wars for many generations, and the Church has taken into celibacy many more of our best, we have been breeding for poor quality for a long time and now show the results. This we think is too facile an explanation; others too have had their heavy casualties over many generations without any such result.

The trouble has been ascribed by some to our type of religion, or the way we use it, performing our bare religious duties almost mechanically, conforming to the customs at births, marriages and deaths, but without passion, without devotion, social duty, often thought of as really women's business.

Again others have suggested that the peculiarities of our constitution make much of our difficulty, but surely we should be capable of making any necessary changes if that is an important factor in our frustration.

This disability of our government is now hitting us where it hurts, in our prestige among the nations, but up to now we have found no easy way to regain our stature as a "great power," and perhaps that is the biggest factor in our trouble. We want an easy way; we don't want to tighten our belts or pay heavy taxes, or reduce our alcoholic intake. Let the next generation worry about such uncomfortable necessities. We can go on a while longer blaming our political enemies, inside or outside our country, and meanwhile live as pleasantly as we can.

Some of us say frankly that we are not sufficiently self-disciplined to be able to make a democracy function sensibly, but we could never return to a monarchy and we have had tastes of dictatorships which were still worse.

Some aspects of our difficulties have now become matters for concern and discussion in the United Nations, particularly our colonial problems. The easy way we took of declaring our most troublesome colonies part of Metropolitan France was a gesture which has not seemed to convince anyone but ourselves that they have been or will be "liberated." People ask such questions as "Are the native people of North Africa free to live on the French Riviera?" or "Can all the people in these Metropolitan Districts vote?"

How can we learn to be reliable, responsible and mature?

Germany

We, the people of a divided nation, are living in such varying and complex emotional and political situations that none of us can speak with confidence for us all. The intense drama through which we have lived during the past more than forty years has left its mark deeply impressed in our personalities. The arbitrary division of our country, decided at Yalta without consulting any of us, has proven as unfortunate for us and for Europe, perhaps for the world, as we knew and predicted it would. Our economy has been torn apart; the position of what was our capital, now isolated in the Communist-controlled East, is felt to be intolerable. Its inhabitants are not sharing, or if at all only to a minor degree, in the booming industrial revival of the West. Our relatives in the East are controlled and almost hopeless. Though few of them support their government, the proportion is probably increasing, largely as the result of such great numbers of those against the regime escaping to the West, but partly because we all tend to submit to authority.

Reunification is increasingly ardently desired by almost all of us. That desire could become so demanding that we would pay any, or almost any, price for its satisfaction. Many of us would be willing to compromise extensively with communism if that would re-establish our unity. There is real danger that, under this great emotional pressure, we might overlook the fact that communism cannot really be compromised with, but only resisted entirely or surrendered to.

Many of us have been, and still are, fearful of the possible consequences of our rearmament. In the past, civilian control of our armed forces has always been precarious. Authoritarianism has been taught widely as the first moral principle and we are inclined to submit to discipline and orders far more easily than to rational discussion and common agreement. Deeply almost all of us like to "know where we stand," know who is superior to us and who inferior, know clearly our position in the "pecking order" which we have regarded as inherent in human relations.

Many of us still do not believe entirely in democracy, though most of us are willing, tentatively, to experiment with it. At the same time we have our fingers crossed, and whether democracy in our country could survive a heavy strain, a major depression, for example, is very doubtful. Some political groups still represent continuing loyalties to long-held German faith in authority. We do not give up our loyalties easily and Protestantism, communism, Roman Catholicism and Germanism, though allied often one with another for purposes of temporary expediency, have not yet really found stable and peaceful ways of living together.

Economically the Western, free part of our country is doing very well. We are re-establishing our old markets, expanding them and developing new ones. We are doing this even in direct competition with the highly industrialized powers which suffered little devastation during the war and have been, from a trade point of view, so far ahead of us since, under Hitler's leadership, or drive, we sacrificed everything for the hope of power. This great success is rapidly outweighing the humiliation of our military defeat and begins to appear to those of us who were brought up to be power-hungry, and have not outgrown that teaching, to offer hope of finally establishing our "place in the sun." This time, though, it will be by way of the now more respectable and acceptable "economic imperialism" rather than by military conquest. Economic expansion, economic nationalism, may yet give us much of what we were looking for when we followed Hitler.

India

We, the people of a nation, are increasing by some five million or more a year. This is the most important and dangerous problem facing us, as our Prime Minister has stated repeatedly. So far only few of us realize the danger deeply, not nearly enough of us to affect favorably our high birth rate. Our excellent governmental health services are keeping a greater and greater proportion of our babies alive, to reproduce in their turn after only a few years. Government is making very extensive efforts to educate our people in their responsibility and obligation to have less children and is doing what it can to teach the use of available methods of birth control, but we are still losing ground. All our enormous efforts to increase production are not keeping up with our population increase. We most urgently need better methods of birth control, which, to be effective, would have to be very cheap, safe, efficient, and not interfere with normal sexual relations.

Fortunately we have no extensive resistance in our country to the use of birth control, but in this vital field Western science has not yet been able to help us significantly. Many of us wonder whether this danger to us and to the cause of democracy is sufficiently realized in Europe and America. We believe this problem to be at least as important as the atomic bomb or atomic energy.

Other very difficult problems also complicate our growth toward economic independence. One of these is the attitude of most of our people toward other forms of life. Belief in rebirth in other such forms is common among us, as is the sacredness of the cow and the monkey. Though they destroy enormous amounts of food, cows and monkeys, to most of us, must be treated with respect and allowed that indulgence. There is no value whatever in other people telling us, as they sometimes do, that we should give up these ancient and illogical attitudes. Some of us know that we should be much better off without these and other handicaps of the same type, but it is politically impossible for any government of our country to take any effective and sudden steps in that direction. Of course it is true everywhere that whenever anything has been taught to small children as sacred, or taboo, a later rational approach cannot be expected to be effective.

Government, following the leadership of our beloved and revered Mahatma Gandhi, has done its utmost to eradicate our old rigid caste system, and with a considerable degree of success. That could not have been done, however, without the patient teaching in which Gandhi had persisted for many years previously.

Volume of population, poor nutrition, disease, illiteracy, ignorance, multiplicity of languages, inadequacy of communication, of roads, of railways, of pure water, of sewage disposal, and their consequences in the low levels of productivity of our people are all problems which reinforce each other, and which together account for much of the apparent inertia of our nation.

Another factor has some importance in our present situation. For many years, while occupied by a foreign power, our accepted role was to criticize, even to sabotage by passive, and sometimes violent, resistance. Very few of us were in positions where we regarded constructive effort as our responsibility. Suddenly, with the establishment of our political independence, our customary attitudes became no longer appropriate. We needed large numbers of determined and constructive people, capable of thinking in general terms, of overriding difficulties, of sacrificing personal values for general good, and of concentrating on and developing areas of agreement. Unfortunately many of us had habitually indulged in carping criticism, argued insignificant detail *ad nauseam,* magnified our minor disagreements, in effect knew only how to be "in opposition," and at that in relation to a very tolerant government. The necessary shift to decisive, responsible and constructive attitudes has not been easy for many of us.

The moral obligation we all feel to provide jobs, trade or any possible economic advantage for all our relatives, whenever we are in a position to do so and before even considering the qualifications of any strangers (called "nepotism" by foreigners), is only very gradually weakening. Though, intellectually, many of us realize that this old pattern is a handicap to our efficiency and to our high intentions for our country, our consciences, and our relatives, reproach us whenever we are disloyal to the old custom. This "nepotism" is largely responsible for the greatly inflated staffs of government departments and of many industries and increases the cost of administration considerably.

We have been singularly fortunate in our Prime Minister, whose leadership has almost invariably been constructive, farsighted and, from our point of view, wise. "Colonialism" is still our greatest fear, as it is for many of the countries around us, whether the colonial threat be political, economic or military. Even minor persistences of the old colonialism irritate and even infuriate us. Goa, as we feel it an anachronism and an insult to us, has become a very important symbol. Its persistence as a colony suggests to us that "colonialism" may not be really dead and conceivably could again conquer us. This highly emotional reaction is one of the indications that we can hardly yet believe that we are really free; we are still suspicious that some power will try to retain or establish some control over us.

We are not pro-Eastern or pro-Western. We are only mildly social-ist but, except for a very few, not Communist. To us communism just as clearly represents colonialism as any of the great colonial powers ever did, and we will not be dominated by either side or by any nation. We believe ardently in the value of the United Nations, and gradually feel our way toward a more significant place among the nations of the world. We are basically peaceful and would like to live in peace with all peoples, but we will not take directions or instructions from anyone and our loyalty cannot be bought. De-fensive alliances appear to us as traps which would limit our freedom of action and could involve us in disastrous adventures with which we are not in sympathy.

Israel

We, the people of a nation, are devoted to what to us is the great-est cause in the world, and we are sometimes ruthless in its service. We are the "chosen people," and after many centuries of the "wil-derness" we are fulfilling at least part of the ancient prophecy of the homecoming of the tribes, though the Messiah long awaited by many has not yet come to establish his Kingdom on earth.

Other people, who happened recently (and indeed for many gen-erations) to be living on our ancient tribal land, still refuse to admit our right to this once fertile but now denuded little area, though to us that right is self-evident. Did not our remote ancestors settle here —having taken it from some other less potent people, slaughtering their males and enslaving their females under the protection and at the behest of our old tribal God and according to the custom of the time? These recent tenants regard us as aggressors and insist that right is on their side. This we can never accept. We have almost never been able to assimilate or to be assimilated. We have been set apart by our old laws and rituals, which even prevented us from eating with those not of our faith, kept us segregated and made us scapegoats whenever scapegoats were wanted.

In long-past ages we have had a noble tradition of great rebel prophets, each of whom did something to change our picture of our old God, gradually civilizing Him, adding kindliness and forgiveness and even after many centuries universality, the one-God idea. Indeed our concept of God became so virtuous that we had to adopt from the Persians, who were our masters for some hundreds of years, the idea of Satan, to account for all the evil in the world. These ideas have now spread over most of the world, but there is much confusion in it because our history and religion have been grossly twisted and often allowances not made for the evolution in our concept of God over the centuries, led by our great prophets. The God of Jeremiah, and much more the God of Jesus, bears little resemblance to the God of Noah, but many sincere people try to believe in all at once!

Consequently many young minds are confused, even distorted, by being expected to believe in a God both kindly and vengeful, just but punishing for sins of ancestors, placable by ritual, or prayer, yet all powerful and all knowing, the fatherly protector but "leading into temptation," loving all people, but unable to keep his loved ones happy because of some "mysterious ways" ascribed to him, and apparently unable to control the "evil" in which the earliest man indulged in defiance of his creator.

Very little of all this really belongs to our religion in its most developed form, and much of it has been added from entirely outside our faith.

During our centuries of exile our wise men evolved masses of detailed laws, designed to keep our people apart from all others and welded into a tight group for mutual protection. This apartness has been apparently both the cause and the result of our persecution by almost all other peoples. It has increased our anxiety and fear and so has kept us emotionally together, though spread all over the world. It has also kept alive in many of us the belief in our eventual power and triumph, when our now universal God will be accepted over all the earth, and our Messiah will reign from Jerusalem.

Some of us are more concerned with the more practical matters of establishing a viable nation, which will be able to stand on its own feet and in time will be independent of the gifts of our own people throughout the world, and of assistance from other countries and from the United Nations.

We are making this barren land again "a land flowing with milk and honey" but we must have help from outside our narrow boundaries. We are determined to enlarge those boundaries at whatever cost of lives is necessary.

We are richly endowed with technically qualified people from many countries, and if allowed to do so could assist the people around us greatly in their economic and social development. We have also many ignorant, illiterate, relatively uncivilized people, but we are rapidly educating and training them for effective co-operation in our cause.

We buy machines from America, oil from Venezuela, timber from equatorial Africa, and anything we sell we must also sell at great distances.

We must have more water; our coastal water table is lowering dangerously as we pump from it for irrigation. Economically our situation is desperate, but we have great resources of devotion and determination and we have long practice in living on very little when necessary.

Some of us, but particularly among those of us who are not living in the ancient homeland, have grown beyond the old tribal and even universal God concept and are not happy about this new revival of our old nationalism. We begin to see that it might be better to have less nations than more in the world. We are not at all sure that separateness on the basis of our old belief that we were God's chosen people is a good thing for us or for the world. Some of us even think that general mutual assimilation of and by all humans into one race without organized distinctions might be best for all of us. We have been held together, and apart from others, for many centuries by fear, a fear induced by our very apartness. Perhaps if we stopped being apart, after only a relatively little while we need not fear. This concept is still regarded with horror, as shameful and traitorous, by most of our people.

Most of us believe that if the nations around us will only accept the fact of our existence and recognize that we can be useful to them here as a nation with them, we can prove our usefulness and eventually develop an economy that will be self-supporting and valuable to the world.

Japan

We, the people of a nation, are in a desperate situation. While we can live on very little we cannot see where sufficient food to keep all our people alive is to come from, unless people of other nations will buy far more of our manufactured goods than they do now. We tried, at a moment that seemed propitious, to expand and make room for ourselves in relatively underdeveloped areas around us, following the pattern of all great nations which have taken over the lands of weaker people throughout history. We had been told by our military men that our forces were invincible and, without experience except against relatively primitive, poorly supplied and corrupt forces, we believed them. We found that we were not strong enough, that suicidal devotion was no match for the power of unlimited raw material and machines.

During recent generations particularly, and continuously for perhaps two thousand years or more, our people have been held together by the Royal Family and its reputed divine origin. For many centuries we have enthusiastically adopted, and adapted, foreign ways. From India, from Korea, from China and more recently from Europe and America, we have taken over religions, ideas, organizational patterns, educational methods, manufacturing techniques and very many other foreign developments. Many of these ways are inconsistent with many of our own older ways, which still persist, though they are even inconsistent with each other in many cases, but we hope in time to attain a more integrated culture.

Much of our economy, since our defeat, has been supported by the victors, and also by vast amounts of money spent in our country as a base for United Nations police action in this region. Our population has grown and is growing at a frightening rate. In our desperation we have had to legitimize surgical abortion, but we are still dependent upon foreign aid for protection from the chaos which would follow the threatened breakdown of our economy. Nothing but greatly increased exports can save us, and the world, from the common threat of such a breakdown. We can export vast amounts

of well-manufactured goods, but almost everywhere steps are taken
to limit buying from us with the cry of "unfair competition" because
of our low standard of living. But how can we raise our standard of
living if we cannot sell abroad? We do not have enough arable land
to feed our people, nor enough raw materials to feed our factories.
We must buy abroad, but we must also sell abroad. Whoever will
buy from us inevitably is our friend, and we will be strongly impelled
to go along with that friend politically. We are accused of black-
mailing Western countries, but can anyone expect us just to die of
starvation, or kill off large numbers of our people? We have been
willing to export our surplus population but no one will accept them.

Having renounced military aggression we ask the wealthy and
well-fed nations, in pursuit of their own stated principles as set out
in the constitution of the United Nations, to help us in the only constructive way possible, by buying our goods. No government can survive in our country unless it can find markets for our manufacturers
so that we can buy food for our people.

We are doing all that we can to educate our people toward having
fewer children and to provide methods of birth control that will be
acceptable to our people. However, significant results from these
programs can hardly be expected in less than a generation or so and
in the meantime our situation is desperate.

South Africa

We, the people of a nation, though a member of a great family of
free nations, are trying, as some of us see it, to go against the main
current of human development in the world. Under the domination
of some of our white minority, we are moving in directions which
sooner or later can produce bloody revolution. Some of us believe
that we are carrying out the intention of our God in making the
colored people our "hewers of wood and drawers of water" and we
are convinced that colored people are not fit for education or social
responsibility. Also the prosperity of our present system depends on
their cheap labor in our mines and fields, and we are determined to
force their subjection to our rule.

Most of us have not yet begun to realize the strength of the world
opinion which is turning against us. We do not admit any fault in the

embarrassment we are causing all the other members of the Commonwealth. Many of us who could not tolerate the bigoted doctrines which have become our government policies have left, or will yet leave, for more congenial and less dangerous countries. Daily the hate and desperation of our colored people rise, and we take more and more repressive measures for securing our heritage and maintaining the principle of "white supremacy." Our extensive trials for "treason," more and more of us begin to see, might as well be called trials for "heresy," and we are increasingly frightened by the obstinate and ruthless policies of our government.

It is questionable whether we can remain in the United Nations as a member of that community of nations. Pressure against our policies is rising and being voiced more and more strongly and impatiently. In spite of that pressure we are determined to take over and absorb into our country adjacent territories, entrusted to our administration by the United Nations and the United Kingdom. Most of the white minority of one of those territories, largely composed of people like ourselves and of Nazi sympathizers, will support our segregation policies and help to enlarge the reactionary island in which we live in an unsympathetic world.

Those of us who are elected to the legislature by the very small minority of the population we allow to vote have shut our eyes to the inevitably disastrous future, as we have been trained to do from infancy in our fanatical and outdated religious education. Of course, we can find justification for all our attitudes in the Bible, which we take as the direct, revealed word of God, which must not be questioned by any mere human. Granted that original premise, there is no possible argument against our attitudes and policies, so there is no common ground for discussion between us and reasonable people. We are building a heritage of terror and death for our children, but it is supported and justified by our stanch faith in the teaching of some of our elders and clergy.

South and Central America

We, the people of a large group of republics, are struggling toward political maturity. We are a very mixed lot, and in that mixture of races and cultures perhaps lies much of our potential value to the world. Some of us have shown that diverse racial, color and cultural groups can assimilate each other to the advantage of all. This is a lesson yet to be learned by most of the people of the world.

Politically we have a tendency toward authoritarianism. Perhaps that tendency is fostered by our childhood upbringing, which is largely controlled by a highly authoritarian religion. From infancy we are taught not to think in any terms of cause and effect; the church presumes to do our basic thinking for us. It follows that we can obey or rebel, and some of us go one way and some the other, but few of us dare to think independently. Democracy, to be effective, requires a large proportion of people who are able to think beyond orthodoxies and loyalties to persons or faiths, and relatively few of us can do that. We are among that company of politically backward countries whose people predominantly adhere to any fixed and authoritarian faith, but we are learning, and increasing numbers of us tire of religious and political dictatorship and intrigues, often with foreigners, for power and the profits of exploitation. Also we are no longer to be, nor resigned to continuing to be, a storehouse of natural resources to be used when convenient by Europe or North America.

More than a hundred years ago our great liberator, Bolívar, freed us from foreign domination, but we have been providing our own dictators much of the time since then. Most of us have yet to develop beyond concern for our own prestige, or that of some political group which is in power or trying to attain power.

Because of the instability of most of our governments and the spoils system under which governments employ their supporters, most of our officials are part-time workers, keeping one foot in some more dependable position or business. This situation is a great handicap, and reduces the efficiency of our governments' offices very seriously; but because of the common practice of political intrigue by officials, and the insecurity of dictators or of governments elected by some type of chicanery, the groups in power almost invariably try to surround and protect themselves by people whose loyalties they have bought. Of course, bought loyalties can usually be sold again to a higher bidder, and hence much of our political trouble.

Some of us begin to see that until we can help our children to establish true cause-and-effect relations in their own thinking, there is little hope for more mature political method in our countries. In the meantime our people suffer unnecessarily, from widespread poverty, malnutrition, ignorance and exploitation, and some of our people profit greatly from those same conditions.

In some of our countries the people have learned that civil riot and assassination are no longer appropriate political methods. We are gradually learning from our own mistakes and, in recent years, many of us have learned much from our associations with representatives of other governments at international meetings, notably in those of the United Nations and its specialized agencies. We have recently discovered that, whenever we can agree sufficiently among ourselves, our votes in the United Nations, used as "the Latin American Bloc," can always get us attention and consideration, and even ardent wooing by powerful international interests. A few of us, doubting a little our ability to use our new position wisely and for world good, become somewhat concerned lest we misuse this new-found power.

Some of us are learning more and more to deal with the realities rather than with the form. The substance of our speeches and our writings is gradually becoming recognized as more important than the oratory or the literary style.

The United Kingdom of Great Britain and Northern Ireland

We, the people of a nation, are gradually becoming better liked, or perhaps only less disliked, in many parts of the world, partly because we are not as strong relatively as we used to be, but partly because we have learned much in centuries of administration over much of the earth's surface.

We have learned, slowly and painfully, the difficult art of compromise. We follow strict rules in things that do not matter, the field of symbols, protocol, heraldry, ritual and pageantry, but not in the important areas of politics, business, administration and international relations. We have also learned that prestige is to be gained by "saving face" for other people, not with a big stick only, though we still use the big stick when interests we regard as vital to our national existence or status are threatened.

We have evolved a form of democracy which suits us, with all the sentiment, love of pageantry and emotion of our peoples focused on the monarchy, a carefully built up and guarded symbol of stability. Consequently our politics and our Parliament are relatively free of the hysteria, hero worship, invective and frenzy found in so many other political systems. Our politicians, no matter how eminent, need no guards, are not followed about by photographers or crowds of the curious. They can play golf or shop in Woolworth's unnoticed. They are just people who work, and work hard, for the government. Sometimes it seems to us that some of them are working harder for their own political party than for us all, but that cannot go too far without offense to our voters.

The loss of almost all our foreign investments in carrying the staggering costs of two world wars left us in a highly precarious situation economically, but we are recovering and looking forward with hope that extensive use of atomic power may lower the high cost of production enforced by our lack of raw materials. We hope we have lost some of our smugness. With some usually elderly exceptions, we are no longer "colony minded" and are preparing all our remaining colonies for increased and eventual complete independence, but too slowly to suit some and too quickly to please others.

Our family of nations is unique in the world. Its members are completely free; there are no constitutions or rules of procedure between us. We have simply decided to live peacefully and co-operatively together with a common symbol for most of us in the monarchy.

The members of this family have assumed no obligations whatever to each other except such as are open to any other country. Obligations left over from our colonial era are vanishing rapidly with political development.

Many of us recognize anachronisms in our lives. The undemocratic and largely hereditary upper house in our legislature is not apparently useful as a symbol to us, but it is deeply planted in our tradition and its members are almost invariably trained from youth for responsible citizenship at that level. It does not lack for ability, interest or industry, but there is some question whether or not the expense is really justified.

Much criticism is heard of our established church and its privileges and rights. Many of us are against it, but it carries much of the burden of respectability we all admire so much, and really interferes very little with important matters. It has become very tolerant, indeed, so much so that there is now more ritual than orthodoxy. Some of us think of it as a comfortable old watchdog, useful in its day, and still able to bark, but with few teeth left. In course of time it will die, but we should be ashamed to do anything to hasten its demise.

We hope that by living in the present and the future our past dominant world-power position will not handicap our continuing development, as it has done other great powers in the past. There are, however, some of us who have begun to feel that we may be well advised to stop trying to be a "great power," with the enormous expense necessary to that status, to reduce our population by exporting whole industries with all the people depending on them, to stabilize our population at the point where we can feed ourselves from our own production of foodstuffs, to reduce our overseas commitments greatly, and, after a transitional period, settle down to a relatively comfortable existence, perhaps in some such pattern as that of Denmark or Sweden, though we do not have the iron Sweden has. Whether or not these attitudes will gain or lose ground we cannot know at this time, but the presenting of these ideas as possibly desirable is forcing widespread reconsideration of our traditional values and loyalties—which is a good thing.

The new field of development of atomic energy could conceivably rejuvenate our economy and make it possible for us to compete successfully for another generation or so, until less-developed countries catch up in that field also. By that time, however, world economy may have grown up to world responsibility, and international competition of the present ruthless type become obsolete.

The United States of America

We, the people of a nation, are very prosperous. We own, or use while we are gradually paying for, enormous amounts and varieties of things. Many of these things must be discarded, often before they are paid for, and replaced by new models, because our advertisers shame us by telling us that last year's models are obsolete, and because ownership of more and more expensive things is for us a socially necessary evidence of our "success."

Dimly some of us begin to realize that our consumption of raw material, soil, water, minerals, oil, even land space, is at a level impossibly prodigal from the point of view of other peoples. We can maintain that level only as long as we can keep for ourselves an excessive share of the limited space of this little planet, obtain far more than our share of raw materials from other peoples, keep out many of the finished products they would like to sell us so they could live a little more as we do, and at the same time sell them ever increasing volumes of the things we manufacture. Often these are not things they need for their own development, but the surplus of our production. We, or at least some of us, know those other peoples have no need of Coca-Cola, they need more nutritious foods; or of flashy automobiles, they need something much more practical and cheap like the early Ford on which we were raised. They certainly could develop better without our gangster movies, though at least these have the pleasing effect for many peoples of making them feel very superior to us and our "way of life."

Many of us earnestly believe that all people everywhere else would give anything they have to be allowed to come and live here in "God's country."

We are very rich and very powerful, and we have been frightened systematically by our national administrations for years, and have developed a degree of fear of outsiders, of anyone different from ourselves, that is not believable to people in other lands. They believe, almost without exception, that our tremendous military preparation, our spy hunting, our panic over subversives, our very real fear that another Communist might get into our country, are masks for aggressive intentions.

We have given vast gifts to those peoples who are in need, at least to those of them who are on our side, but we insist on giving most of our assistance directly, so that we are sure we will get the credit, rather than through international agencies set up largely for that purpose. Actually, of course, our method of giving only adds to the suspicion of our motives which we meet everywhere, but we are convinced that our methods of supply, of distribution, of technical assistance, are far more efficient than those of international specialized agencies employing experts from many countries. Also we are

afraid that some of the services would go to people whose attitudes
we do not approve.

Some few of us begin to suspect that we have a horse-and-buggy
type of governmental system, useful in its day, but not at all what
is needed in this world of rapidly changing circumstances. Some of us
who have attended meetings of international organizations as delegates of our country have learned much. We have experienced bewilderment and frustration, and we have seen how we bewilder and
frustrate delegates from other countries who may be earnestly and
sincerely trying to co-operate with us. Sometimes they try to explain
to us how they feel we let them down so frequently. They say they
never know where we stand, what our policy is; indeed it seems to
them that our policies are often only temporary expediencies and
often determined more by local political circumstances at home than
by the realities of the world situation with which we are supposed to
be dealing.

We are not able to negotiate as can other delegations because we
have no authority ourselves and we have none to appeal to. If a new
situation arises, other delegates can cable or telephone their foreign
ministers or the cabinet minister concerned and get an answer,
usually within a few hours, that can be stated publicly as the policy
of their government. When we are asked what our policy is, we have
sometimes to stall; the most we can get from our administration at
home is often a warning not to commit ourselves because of the mood
of our Congress, or sometimes we are told of an "administration
policy which will be recommended to Congress." If we quote that in
a meeting we are asked when a decision will be reached, and we
have no answer. It may take months or years and in the meantime
we must abstain from voting, or in some other way leave the rest
of the world uncertain about whether we are with them or not.

One of the most unfortunate results of this disability is the embarrassment it causes our best friends. Our antagonists are always very
happy about our obvious uncertainties, and they like to indicate their
understanding and sympathy for us in our having to get along with
what they regard as an irresponsible legislature and an impotent
administration.

We had never recognized the extreme rigidity and cumbersomeness of our methods of checks and balances until we saw the relative ease with which other governments can change their attitudes or methods to adjust themselves to rapidly changing circumstances. Some of them are even able to do things just because they are sensible, and for the general good. Some delegations even come to international meetings with broad terms of reference and plenipotentiary powers to commit their governments.

We seem to be controlled by old rules made under greatly different circumstances by men wise in their time and place, but with no experience of the world as it is now.

We have come to expect that unless watched continually our officials will indulge in nepotism and graft and political machinations, as indeed they often do, so we set up complicated systems of checks, with investigating committees and pseudolegal machinery and secret reports. We have developed a very extensive secret police because we have been so frightened by communism, with which many of us associate intellectualism, atheism, homosexuality and all manner of other perversions, but apparently we are now over the most extreme degree of that phase.

Of course, other governmental systems have their handicaps in international relations, but ours affect the lives of so many hundreds of millions of the world's people that they are far more important to the world, and to ourselves, than the disabilities of other governments.

That our international value is minimal during the year of a presidential election, that is to say, about one quarter of the time, is widely recognized. Elections at home seem to outweigh the importance of the whole world, and yet they are commonly conducted in a highly emotional, even hysterical, atmosphere. The antics of some of our senators and congressmen are matter for world-wide jokes and cartoons. Their lack of specific education for their legislative jobs is a constant wonder to other peoples.

Unprepared as we have been, we have been precipitated, largely by two world wars, into the position of the most economically powerful nation to exist in the world. Individually, many of us, and particularly many of our civil servants, are doing everything possible to carry our great world responsibilities with dignity and devotion to the common good. Individually, many of us are highly regarded by representatives of foreign governments and by people all over the world who know us, but almost universally our political organization is regarded as antiquated and inadequate for the functioning of a great nation in the world as it is now. This attitude is so common throughout the world, outside our own borders, that it demands our attention. The facts should be examined, not in the light of our carefully inculcated loyalties to our constitution and our "way of life," but in the cold, clear light of an objective scientific approach.

We, in common with other nations, have expressed our good intentions in the constitutions of the United Nations and of its specialized agencies. Now we need to examine our Constitution, our political organization, our administrative methods and relationships, our government institutions and our ways of doing business, in the light of those expressed intentions. What should we change if we really intend to live co-operatively on a world basis?

The Union of Soviet Socialist Republics

We, the people of a nation, are under the spell and compulsion of a prophetic vision, which a few of us begin to see is drawn in long-obsolete patterns, and which has yet to make much more misery and perhaps death on this planet. Our prophet believed that the expressions of human nature of people belonging to some social classes could not be changed except by violence and absolute controls. That belief has enslaved millions and slowed the social development of our people. Technically the controls imposed have produced marvels in an amazingly short time; our production of the first "earth satellite" emphasizes that fact; But we tend, as almost everyone else did a few generations ago, to see everything in absolute terms, black or white, good or bad, for us or against us. When we do seem to compromise it is often not a true compromise, but only tactical maneuvering in order to gain our own ends.

We trust no one, because that has been our training. We bend all thinking, science, art, literature, everything, to our long-term purpose, the ascendancy of our way of life, which we believe to be desirable for all people, and inevitable sooner or later for all the world.

Some of us, particularly some of us who have had contacts outside our own country, have some hope that our orthodoxy may soften with time and are sometimes unhappy about attitudes expressed by our government but not shared by most of our people. Slowly we are learning from our mistakes, but our hierarchy, like all authoritarian systems, can allow us to change only very slowly. At least we know now that there is no profit to our cause or to our prestige in open warfare with our opponents. Some of us believe, or at least hope, that the capitalist countries will learn to live co-operatively, as we hope we too may learn in time. When they, and we, do so our differences will become insignificant.

Some of us recognize the fact that we are only just recently coming out of the Middle Ages. It would be helpful if other peoples looked at their own ancestors, at a comparable stage of their development, for a better understanding of many of our behavior patterns.

We tend to attribute Machiavellian complexities, deep-laid plans and long-range motives to our opponents when some of us begin to realize that often they are not expressing more than local political expediencies, quite irrevelant to the world situation and often against their own real interests. An apt illustration is the gangster movies which they sell to us and which we use to show our peoples the way of life of Western countries. It had been thought by some of us that these movies must have been planned to corrupt us in some way, but it appears that the only real motive is the earning of money. We are very happy to co-operate, but are astonished that any people would blacken their own culture so effectively for the sake of minor amounts of money. We, naturally, do not complain because they provide us at negligible cost with propaganda against their way of life far more effective and cheaper than anything we could make for ourselves, but we cannot respect their sense of values, or their intelligence, or their governmental system, whichever is responsible for this type of windfall for us.

For long we believed their foreign policies were planned also for specific world purposes, but gradually we have become convinced they are commonly determined by group or political party pressures and represent internal expediencies only. Consequently we have learned that we can produce confusion in the enemy camp by the simple ruse of announcing sudden changes in our own attitudes, and then, before their ponderous methods can establish an agreed reaction, changing our ground again. With our system, of course, this type of tactical maneuvering is very simple and very easy, and does not make any permanent commitments for us whatever.

We earnestly believe that we do have an obligation to do what we can to disturb the "decadent imperialistic countries." We have a real faith that sooner or later their systems will break down, that they will see the light, and will become one with us, naturally under our leadership, which at our present stage of development means under our control.

III.

Implications

WE CANNOT claim any scientific validity for these random observations about certain of the feelings, attitudes and situations of some
of the peoples of a few countries. We must recognize that every
observation we have made, or may make, is incomplete and to be
accompanied by many reservations and exceptions. Perhaps the chief
value of such observations as we have tried to make, or indeed any
value, is as an exercise for ourselves in getting outside our usual and
accidental environment, that framework which, unless we check
ourselves very frequently, we tend to take as a standard or valid
pattern from which everything worth seeing can be seen, and seen
truly. Actually everything we see from inside any one subculture or
culture will be distorted out of true perspective or untruly colored.

Any culture is, basically, just a particular set of attitudes, of points
of view, of original premises, of fixed relative values. These stereotypes are very useful in saving us from having to think everything
out for ourselves. Without such common agreements among groups
of people there could be no organized society, only social chaos.
Whenever our remote ancestors banded together even temporarily
for hunting, for common protection or more effective aggression, to
keep fire going or for any other purpose, areas of agreement about
behavior had to be found. Without such agreement there could be
no effective co-operation, and man has had to co-operate to survive
as have had many other forms of life, particularly the individually
more defenseless. The gregarious animals, like the dog, bee, ant,
elephant, man and many birds, use social organization and group
and self-discipline as a weapon and a method of effective competi-

tion. Wherever the rules for such co-operation have become so rigid that appropriate adjustments to meet changing circumstances become very difficult, as in man's pattern of nationalism, for instance, co-operation with other groups may become almost impossible.

At the present time co-operation irrespective of national or cultural boundaries is essential for the very survival of the race. Most of us, however, have been brought up inside one culture; only the exceptionally fortunate have had any other experience in their early, most important, years of development. Now we find that we must learn how to live co-operatively with many kinds of people whose stereotypes, taboos, attitudes, scales of relative values, etc., are outside our experience, just as ours are commonly outside theirs. Even if intellectually we know about each other's peculiarities, we tend to regard ours as standard and right and theirs as mistaken or even evil. This is a very real problem, and in the new kind of world in which we live now we cannot count on survival of our race unless we can solve it far more successfully than ever before in human history. We must all learn that attitudes or customs are not necessarily good just because they were imposed on us as children and seem normal to us.

Fortunately every person, no matter in what part of the world he happens to live, and providing only that he can observe and think independently, can do something to soften the prejudices he meets around him, and particularly to help children to free themselves a little of their cultural certainties. This is one area in which governments can only follow their people; the real job has to be done in the homes of the world.

Among all these people we find many similarities and many differences. We find prejudices, traditional attitudes and old faiths (many of them much distorted in the interests of the power and wealth of their hierarchies; for instance what would Jesus, that antiritualist, have thought of the attitudes of many of those who presume to represent Him now?); rigidities based on the certainties of ancestors, often irrelevant now; exclusive loyalties to groups; hate or fear of people or ideas because they are different; deep anxiety over most of the earth, really about ourselves, but always seen as fear of loss of control of some other people. We find urgings to return to obsolete faiths, or rigid conformity, or narrow nationalism, or "preventive" aggression or vast national armaments.

Having recognized all these factors, active in our world now, we may well wonder what can be done about this highly unsatisfactory, complex and difficult situation. Doing our best to look at all social systems as though free of loyalty to any of them, which would we choose, if any? It would seem that most or all of them have some attractive elements. What should be our criteria? We find a very common reason for acceptance in tradition, the pattern in which one happened to be born, quite independently of whether that pattern is still valid in changed circumstances. The customs of the natives, that is to say, our own customs, become sacred just because they were imposed on us as right and "normal" when we were small children and were incorporated into our consciences. That commonly happens not as an overt act, but simply by omission, by not being shown in childhood that our local and temporary customs are really just that, and not universal or necessarily of permanent value. Of course, we should not allow that accident of early environment to affect our judgment now that we are grown up.

Also common are rebellion against authority and acceptance of patterns just because they defy traditional values, ardent search for prestige and power, drive toward successful competition to get ahead of other people, as an individual or as a group, the "class struggle"; demands for opportunity to suppress other people who think or act differently; insistence on complete freedom for the individual, often to the extent of freedom to limit the freedom of others. We find loss of faith in one religion or social system and searchings for a better magic to avoid the difficulties and pain of thinking for oneself, and very often we see earnest people wanting to "do the right thing" to "help the world" but so commonly, because of early training, looking for some supernatural path toward that end.

All these and more are the apparent reasons for the highly emotional loyalties we see supporting great varieties of social patterns. Occasionally we may find a mature, thought-out conviction, relevant to the real world's situation and not resting on the accident of tradition, local loyalty or self-seeking. Such convictions can be and are usually presented clearly and simply and free of mysticism, though taking account of its presence and importance to most people. They are also free of special concern for the welfare of any particular group.

If we look at all religious faiths as though we were coming into this world for the first time, that is to say, free of the prejudices we normally carry as the result of the accident of the time and the place of our birth and early environment, would we choose one of them, and if so, which one? The choice is very wide; there are hundreds of sects and cults of Christianity alone. What should we use as criteria for such a selection? We may hear many reasons quoted for acceptance of this or that religion or sect. They make a long list. Some of them are social value for the world, whether or not we need or want it for ourselves; most amazing miracles; comfort value for ourselves; promises of most delights in a life after death; most beautiful or impressive ritual; evening up of happiness in this world and another future life; opportunity eventually to be free of the burden of life in merging with some vague infinite; feeling of identification with power, or wealth, and consequent feeling of superiority over other peoples; assurance of security for one's own soul and freedom from fear of torment, the fryings and boilings and toastings and other painful procedures awaiting the "unsaved"; fear of losing the respect or protection of our departed ancestors; most devoted worship of a loving God; most hopeful of answers to prayers for our own advantage, of health, of fortune, of security, of soul; opportunity to lay aside adult and mature responsibility and leave our thinking to the authority of ancient soothsayers or prophets or contemporary hierarchy; just tradition, intellectual laziness or timidity, resignation to the accident of time and place and family of birth and early environment; the best offer of something to lean on, to shelter behind, from our human loneliness in a vast and none too friendly universe; social pressure, also the accident of time and place, reluctance to offend the faithful no matter how absurd the faith; claims of exclusive truth, based on authoritarian interpretation of old writings.

Which of all these or other reasons command our acceptance of, and allegiance to, the many available faiths, or could any of them? Would we want to accept any of them if we were free of all previous ties?

Along with any of these could we accept feast or fast days; circumcision, male and/or female; taboo on various kinds of food and drink and behavior, permanent or on some prescribed days; confession of our offenses against their laws to designated members of hierarchies, and acceptance of their punishment; obedience to the "revealed truth" as presented by elected or appointed authorities; complex and onerous rituals of praise and obedience represented as pleasing or placating an anthropomorphic god; necessity of performing long pilgrimages or repeating prescribed prayers at prescribed times; or many other "duties" of the faithful?

We might well look briefly at this phenomenon called "faith." To most people, the word means more than just "belief," even more than belief firmly held to the point of certainty. It carries a strong moral connotation. People amend and change their "beliefs" relatively freely, and generally without a feeling of guilt, but "faiths" are much more difficult to change. Any such attempt is commonly labeled and felt as "heresy," "apostasy," or some other term of criticism. Is there a word in the English language, without connotation of blame, for the process of fighting oneself free of an early imposed faith, which in maturity one does not believe because one finds that it is not true? Even language takes for granted the "rightness" of our early belief and the "badness" of dropping it, even if for something better and truer. Of course, if one drops his own faith in favor of *ours* (whatever ours is), he is a convert and "saved" and therefore good and right.

We find almost everywhere a great reluctance on the part of parents, teachers and religious leaders to allow young children to learn about other religions than that of their parents. Many parents seem to be ashamed that they themselves are free of the beliefs imposed upon them as children and are reluctant, especially to their children, to admit that freedom. Of course, in some parts of the world, such reluctance is quite understandable, as in countries like Spain, French Canada, some of the Moslem countries and various other parts of the world. In such places any admission of freedom from religious control might result in social ostracism and even loss of employment. Until recently in human history it might well invite torture and death.

IV.

Anxiety

AS WE explore in these areas of experience beyond our own culture, reminding ourselves again to try to free ourselves of, or at least recognize and discount, our local, national, religious or other cultural prejudices, we find that symptoms of a deep anxiety are apparent in very large numbers of people. Usually it seems that the degree of anxiety felt is grossly out of proportion to the amount of real danger in their actual situation.

We see that anxiety is very common, indeed almost universal, in the human race. It is found in greater or less degree, more or less rationalized by attachment to specific fears, more or less converted into symptoms pointing to heart, blood pressure, digestive, sexual or other bodily functions, or in the social field acting as a potent causal factor behind such signs as instability, alcoholism or drug addiction, mysticism, emotional conversion, fanaticisms, delinquency and criminality, egocentricity, need for power, cruelties, ruthless competition, hero worship, acquisitiveness, limitation of loyalties to national, religious, racial, social, color or other groups, and in many other recognizable ways.

We may well examine this pervasive anxiety more fully. It is not specific for this or that culture, though said to be less evident in certain cultures at certain times. Strangely, from our usual point of view, it is reported that among the Eskimos anxiety has been hardly recognizable, though the rigors and dangers of their lives have been exceptionally severe, but also it is said that, with the encroachment of white culture, of various Christian religions, and of white men's diseases, anxiety is also developing. Such reports should be investigated carefully, because we still have much to learn about anxiety and its causes.

We find also, of course, natural and valid fears of real threats, but these are local, specific and temporary, and perform a useful service in motivating adequate protective procedures in real material terms. They do not produce the pervasive anxiety we are concerned with, which is produced by difficulties inside each personality, internal conflicts and complexes. These arise from feelings of guilt and sin or inferiority or insecurity, unacceptable desires, unknown hates or loves, unrealized rebellions or any such tensions within the personality. Usual complications are beliefs in spirits, gods, saints, devils and other manufactured protectors, enemies, or potential enemies, which can be dealt with only by magic and protective rituals. In this morbid atmosphere anxiety seems to be inevitable and the prescribed protective measures, or their side effects, are rarely if ever for the good of the human race. They do however contribute handsomely to the prestige and power of the dominant few.

A very significant condition apparently essential to the imposing of this load of anxiety on humans seems to be that it be done in childhood and by the authority of parents or substitute parents. It is not usually done directly; indeed most parents probably do not know what they are doing to their children in giving them an early introduction to the concept of sin and guilt and supernatural beings. As though these were not enough, many parents add additional anxiety-breeding burdens, superstitions, astrology, local prejudices and faiths which defy intelligence and paralyze it. Many parents even arrange to have their small children taught things which quite specifically they no longer believe themselves, in Sunday school, for instance. It is somehow thought to be "good" to offer up children to the same intellectually paralyzing influences from which it may have taken their parents many years to effect even a partial escape. This, of course, is the effect of conscience on the parents, that persistent voice which tells us that whatever we believed when we were children is "good," whether true or not!

We might pause here to note that in most people all over the world there is an apparent paralysis or distortion or lack of mature development of the imagination. Imagination, which should be utterly free, seems to have been fenced within boundaries prescribed by parental, religious and civil authority, in homes and Sunday and day schools. There has been a widespread pattern of control and distortion which has robbed most children, and later adults, of the valuable functions of a free and well-developed imagination. One of these functions should be free exploration, unhampered by local taboo, of all possible human experience. Properly developed, that function of imagination is a potent protection against unquestioning belief and immature faiths. It will insist on reasonable evidence for belief and will not be carried away by wishful thinking.

The tendency to believe independently of evidence, or even in defiance of it, once encouraged in a child under trusted parental authority, and strongly protected by conviction of sin and by taboo, can be cured only slowly and painfully and usually only partially. Much of the irrational anxiety in the world seems to be founded on that tendency. Shifts in such faiths are common: it is not hard to be "converted" from one absolute faith to another as long as the new one seems to provide a better protection from anxiety and a reprieve from obligation to think for oneself.

Some of the results of this tendency to believe whatever we learned in childhood may be seen in our common unquestioning faith in our own institutions, often knowing little of any others. In this way we tend to believe in the religion of our family, the constitution of our country, our system of justice, even our ways of doing business, as right and superior to those of any other people, without having studied other religions, other constitutions, other justiciaries or other business methods. Some of us even have the same certainties about our clothes, our haircut, our armed forces, our language or accent, and everything else we have or are. Of course to the extent that we feel and believe in these ways we can hardly be expected to understand, appreciate and co-operate effectively with the other kinds of people, who often feel just the same way about their native customs as we do about ours.

Throughout history whoever has dared to question these early-inculcated faiths has been called heretic, iconoclast, rebel, traitor, Communist, subversive or whatever term will most effectively appeal to the prejudices of the particular time and place. Always it has been clear that, in the interests of keeping control, the unafraid, the un-regimented, should be suppressed whether the suppression is done by parents, teachers, dictatorships or hierarchies.

So we have produced in each generation people taught not to think, but to believe. Of course it is much easier for parents to impose beliefs than to try themselves to think out reasoned answers to their children's intelligent questions. Our own early days of inno-cent questioning, of presinful freedom to think freely, long forgotten, we fasten on our children the same chains of conformity which bind us.

If there is to be hope for freedom from anxiety and fear in the world and for peace, it appears that something will have to be done to discredit faith in favor of reason, and to change the foundation of belief away from its ancient base in tradition, authority, magic, miracle and ritual to a more useful, dependable and reasonable reli-ance on observation, knowledge and intelligence. These are develop-mental areas in which man can go forward and improve the use of his equipment from generation to generation and perhaps even slowly improve his equipment. The old orientation is backward to-ward certainties founded in ignorance, superstition and prejudice. By using his present equipment of knowledge and intelligence, man should be able to take charge of his own earthly destiny far more effectively than by reliance on propitiation of ancient gods, scaring off or running away from ancient devils, or engaging in rituals, fasts or prayers in hope of pleasing or catching the attention or sympathy of some supernatural power. It is clear that man's highest develop-ment, that is, his greatest progress beyond all other forms of life away from our common primitive origin, is in the field of intelli-gence. Faith is a relatively primitive, crude and nonspecific in-strument when dealing with changing circumstances. While man's knowledge was very local and limited, while his environment and conditions of survival were changing relatively slowly, not even noticeably in one or two generations, faith in the attitudes and be-havior patterns of the elders had some real value. Very little was being added contemporarily to the total knowledge available to the tribe. The traditional legends, developed over long periods to try to make the unknowns useful to authority for the gaining of prestige and power, adapted themselves slowly to slow social changes.

As people became more civilized, developed ethics and laws and control of their own behavior, they had to civilize their gods also, though, astonishingly, some people even now, themselves relatively civilized, can worship a god of vengeance, who is insatiable for praise, and can be coaxed or persuaded or placated or pleased by the performance of certain magic rituals. This, of course, is to worship a god far inferior morally, intellectually and socially to ourselves, a frightening illustration of how faith can defy reason.

For many generations thinking people in many places have recognized these facts but generally felt that time was on the side of reason and that with increasing knowledge the ancient and primitive faiths would die out. They could not foresee the appalling increase in man's destructive power that has taken place during the last fifteen years or so, nor the dreadful load of guilt and anxiety now carried by many millions of people because of the other millions they have killed, and are preparing to kill, nor the consequent great risk of a mass retreat from reason back into religious certainty and magic. Circumstances have changed and are changing too fast for the ancient slow evolutionary ways of development by long trial and error, with retreat to the thinking and behavior of the forefathers in the face of serious threat. That way now lies racial suicide.

Man's tremendously increased power to kill, now total and final, while nationalism and military, commercial and political, aggression are still usual; the fearful present rate of increase of world population and man's apparent inability to control it; the widespread anxiety we have noted, now at a dangerous level of tension; the spread of juvenile delinquency—all these among many others are signs and symptoms of our mental and social retardation and of our failure to adjust adequately to greatly changed circumstances.

This is a new kind of world. Its conditions of racial survival were entirely unknown to our forefathers. Like a snake constricted and immobilized by the tightness of its old skin, we are impotent until we can slough off our own old types of controls and emerge in the glory of the full use of our intellectual endowment and the expectation that future generations will develop it far beyond any possibility of our foreseeing or understanding.

Back as far as we know anything of the cultural history of the race we find strong evidences of pervasive anxiety. Specialists have almost always been employed and supported by even small social groups to deal with their anxiety. Witch doctors, shamans, military leaders, priests, soothsayers and oracles have flourished and competed with each other for ascendancy and power throughout the history of this anxiety-ridden race. Their reason for being, their area of operation, and above all their weapon have been anxiety. It has been clear to many thinking people for many generations that without a high level of anxiety there would be no need or demand for magic, for witchcraft, for miracles, for military might, for pleasing or placating of gods, or for a priesthood, hierarchy or general staff. It seems to have been a major concern of the anxietymongers, or at least all that have lasted very long, to feed this anxiety, to nurture it and to promote its growth to as high a level as possible consistent with control by the hierarchy concerned. Extensive investigations should be done to find out whether or not these are valid observations. It is important that we should know all we can about anxiety and its causes. It may be a major factor among those pushing us toward racial suicide.

Because anxiety is clearly one of the greatest barriers to world understanding and co-operation, the United Nations might well ask the World Health Organization, perhaps in co-operation with the World Federation for Mental Health, to undertake long-term studies of anxiety, its causes and possible methods of prevention.

V.

Aggression

THE FEAR of aggression, being attacked, or of being shut in and prevented from expanding, is so widespread in the world, as it has been throughout human social history, that in most cultures, and for a very long time, preparation for defense or offense has been and is a very heavy economic and psychological burden. That burden is common to almost all the peoples of the world, though it weighs more heavily on some than on others. The distinction between the aggression which stems from that anxiety and the aggression which simply uses anxiety as an excuse for a drive for expansion is not always clear. Naturally every aggressor will claim fear of invasion, or of dangerous threat to national interest or existence, or of prevention of his necessary expansion to try to justify his aggression. Such justification is primarily necessary for his own people in order to prepare them for the slaughter to which they must expose themselves in embarking on an aggressive venture.

From the point of view of world opinion, or at least world acceptance, until quite recently aggression, if successful, has been its own justification. The slaughter of Indians in America, or of native Africans, or of many Asiatic peoples, simply because they resisted white or other expansive aggression, or the imposition of a particular religion, has usually been accepted as necessary. The reluctance of all those people peacefully to accept an invasion and domination has been commonly regarded as perverse and wicked, therefore punishable with a clear conscience.

Many of the prosperous people of the world are prone to ignore the fact that, in almost every case, their own comfort is built on the same type of aggression they now forbid to those people who have the misfortune to have been born of less aggressive, or less successfully aggressive, ancestors. For these same prosperous people to talk of territorial justice is regarded as a bad joke by the hungry peoples. Aggression was regarded as admirable when engaged in all over the Americas by the Dutch, English, French, Portuguese and Spanish, and in Africa by the Americans, Belgians, Dutch, English, French, Germans, Portuguese and Spanish, but it was just a little too late when the Italians tried it. Moral styles had changed, not at that time enough to prevent the Italian aggression, but enough to justify forced restitution later on.

Aggression was still respectable when the Americans, Dutch, English, French, Portuguese, were taking territory in Asia and the West and South Pacific, but not by the time Japan was strong enough to take her turn. It is tragic for Japan but fortunate for some others that their attempt did not take place earlier.

There is really no room for a "holier than thou" attitude in those of us whose "superiority" is the result of notably successful aggression by our recent ancestors. To stop the game when, or perhaps because, one is winning heavily is not of itself to be regarded as admirable. Nevertheless, it is clear to most of the world's people that a halt must be called to the old and long-respected system of grabbing territory from weaker people. It is bad luck for the land-poor peoples that they did not grab more land before the rules were changed. Perhaps the lucky people have some responsibility to help to ease the lot of the unlucky ones. Those who would speak of justice in this context must surely recognize such an obligation.

It may be assumed that a nation, that is, a government, cannot take aggressive action against others unless its people will support that action. In the past such willingness to risk life and property might need to be found in only a certain few of the people, such as army leaders and dominant politicians; but now, when aggression invites total destruction of the population, a government will need to be assured of almost universal support from its people before taking such a gamble. Otherwise the government would risk revolution by its own people.

Support for such a venture from a preponderance of the people will depend on various factors. The first and most important condition for such blind following is to be found among people who have been brought up to "believe"; these are people who have learned in childhood to believe that "faith" is more virtuous and admirable than thought. They have been taught to believe in "miracles" as though they were true; in supernatural interventions in man's affairs coming between cause and effect, directly by gods or through the medium of priests or saints or spirits or devils; in the saving of one's own soul as a primary end in life transcending all social values; in "obedience" as a moral principle, or the rightness of the local systems of government, and of business and of marriage, and of all the other local "customs of the natives" into which they might happen to have been born. They have been taught to follow, and to feel selfishly, rather than to think independently and to behave co-operatively with all people.

We have only to observe the uninhibited behavior of small children to recognize that aggression is one of the normal expressions of human nature, which is not to say that its free expression is a good thing or should be allowed in adults in this stage in the world's social development, but its existence in all normal people must be accepted if it is to be understood and dealt with effectively. Influences which tend to increase aggressive pressure in individuals and convert it into its pathological manifestation "hostility," or on the other hand to render it more controllable, need to be identified so that the former may be discouraged and the latter encouraged. There should be no expectation of developing an educational system through homes, schools or religions that will eliminate aggression from human nature, at least not in any predictable time. Selective breeding, even if it could be effective, is certainly not acceptable for free human beings. However, there is much evidence that something can be done to reduce aggressive pressure below the level which has been usual up until now, or to find less dangerous or pathological outlets for its expression.

Already much is known of types of influences which tend to help the normally aggressive infant toward normally aggressive but not hostile maturity, and also of types of influence which tend to leave the same type of infant burdened in adulthood with excessive loads of aggressive necessity and hostility. Of course, there is not complete agreement among psychologists, psychiatrists and experts in child development on these matters; there is still room for much observation, thinking and experiment.

To suggest experiment in development of children is often attacked as inhuman, cold-blooded and indefensible, but in fact all the methods of bringing up children of all times and places should be recognized as experimental no less because large numbers have been or are being treated in the same ways. Except for some methods developed during quite recent years, the present experiments in child development are almost accidental, the results of slow developments of methods often initiated or amended for extraneous reasons, and they have not dealt effectively with aggression.

Upbringing and education have been influenced largely by such considerations as "soul saving" eradication of "sin," prestige of parents, "keeping up with the Joneses," desirability of unquestioning obedience both in behavior and belief, superiority of "faith" over free enquiry, free use of intelligence and weighing of evidence. Most certainly none of these influences is useful in lessening aggression, or in preventing the development of hostile attitudes.

VI.

Population

HAVING glanced at some points of view, some samples of problems of nations, internal and external, it may be useful briefly to remind ourselves of some of the world's problems which cut across national boundaries and affect the welfare, or even survival, of peoples.

High, perhaps highest, on the priority lists of world problems is that of a rapidly expanding world population. The net increase is now about 85,000 a day, something of the order of 30,000,000 a year. That rate is increasing each year.

Modern medicine has made its greatest contribution in saving the lives of infants and small children. As infant mortality is being more effectively controlled, particularly in the less economically developed countries with previously very high infant mortality rates, survival to childbearing age is becoming tremendously more frequent, and a big upsurge in birth volumes and survival rate will probably occur in the very near future. Already, after only a few years of reducing death rates, and in spite of wars, malaria and other still-persisting diseases, some countries find themselves in desperate situations because of their frightening population increases. For example in Japan, about the size of Montana, but with only a small proportion, about 16 per cent, of her rocky and mountainous islands arable, there is a population of about 90,000,000, and it is increasing by more than a million a year. There is no sane hope that Japan's own food production can increase at anything like that rate. The Japanese government reluctantly has had to take the lamentable step of legitimizing surgical abortion for economic reasons, as the lesser of evils. Between three and four hundred thousand such abortions each year hardly begin to deal with the vast problem. What can Japan do? There are various possibilities, starvation and chaos, emigration of at least a million a year, aggressive war, a great and increasing surplus of exports over imports, or really effective birth control throughout the population. These are possible courses for the people of that country.

Resignation to starvation, and the bloodshed that would go with it, is intolerable in this generation. Aggressive war has been tried and failed, as it would fail again. The present economic systems of the world cannot provide greatly expanded and permanently expanding markets for Japanese manufacturers sufficient to feed all their people and provide a rising standard of living. The Communist system may well appear to Japan as the only gamble that offers any chance of survival for millions of her people, unless something effective can be done by the rest of the world to help in these desperate straits. An effective program of birth control, leading to a drastic reduction in birth rate, seems to be the only rational and permanent solution for Japan.

In India the population is increasing by at least five million a year. The government is well aware of this dreadful threat and is conducting an extensive campaign of education and instruction to try to cope with it, but education without adequate methods of birth control is not very effective. Unfortunately, the rhythm system of birth control, depending on periodic sexual abstinence, has been shown by experiments assisted by the World Health Organization and the United Nations to be largely ineffective in an ignorant and superstitious population. The great advantage, and limitation, of that method is that it costs nothing, except self-control. No method depending on the use of costly material is practical in a country where individual economic productivity is as low as in India, but self-control, particularly in the sexual field, is not easily learned.

Surgical abortion in effective numbers is not possible in India because of the costs, insufficient numbers and distribution of the medical profession and hospital facilities, and widespread resistance on the part of the people, whose creed is largely oneness with nature. Attempts are being made to utilize more effectively locally available material for birth control, but so far the results have not appeared to be very encouraging. India needs help with this, the greatest of her problems, which is also the problem of all citizens of the world.

Ceylon, considerably smaller than Maine, with a population of about nine millions, is increasing by at least a quarter of a million a year. Increase in food production cannot keep up with this frightening flow of new babies. Ceylon's excellent public health services are saving more babies' lives than ever before and so far it has been possible to buy food sufficient for a low level of nutrition for the people. Ceylon's rubber export has been the chief money earner to maintain this necessary importation of food. In recent years the choices open to Ceylon's government were to announce to their people that many thousands were to die of starvation, or to sell their rubber to Hong Kong for China. Great pressure came from the U.S.A. in favor of starvation, as no permanent market for Ceylon's rubber was suggested, only an embargo on such exports to China. Of course, no democratic government could choose starvation for its people and survive, and Ceylon took the only possible course, selling its rubber wherever it can, and keeping its people alive. However, no permanent solution has yet been found.

Haiti and Puerto Rico, among Western Hemisphere countries, are in the most serious population difficulties. These are largely Roman Catholic countries, and up to this time widespread misery and malnutrition are increasing and real starvation appears to be inevitable.

Italy also has a chronic surplus of people. It was kept down in the last generation by mass emigration, particularly to North America, but that has now thinned to an ineffectual trickle. The Government of Italy announced, a few years ago, that the rest of the world must accept 600,000 surplus Italians a year if Italy's economy was to be able to support its population. There is no possibility of export of such numbers in the future. The nineteen fifty-four quota of the U.S.A. for Italians was 5,654, and Canada has admitted less than 100,000 in the last five years. The Government of Italy indicates no solution, which means starvation.

With improving public health services and rising population and standards of living, many countries now just able to feed their people, and some which now export food, will be in trouble. Rising standards of living mean more houses and more land used for them, more automobiles and more roads, which, in the modern four- and six-lane versions with wide boulevards, use enormous amounts of land. Much of that land which will have to be used for roads and garages and houses and railways and airports and shopping centers and factories and office buildings is now agricultural land, producing food.

The loss of food-producing land in the next twenty-five years will be very great, but it will also be possible to bring much new land, now desert, under cultivation by extensive irrigation. To be effective, such schemes will require the investment of many billions of dollars in the very near future, and continuously as long as there is any reclaimable land left on the earth. It may be hoped that before all such reserves have been exhausted effective means of stopping population growth may be found.

There is no discernible hope of increasing agriculture, or fisheries, or other food production soon enough or fast enough to prevent many millions now living, or soon to be born, from starving, but much can be done as soon as we, the peoples of the world, are willing to overcome outdated taboos and really take this problem seriously.

In past times, when national security depended on infantry soldiers, there was good reason for governments to take all possible measures to increase their populations. Some, such as Hitler and Mussolini, did everything they could to stimulate production of babies, while they used their excessive populations as an excuse for demanding more room. Is there any longer any national need for larger populations?

Modern weapons of mass destruction, atomic and biological, have rendered man power irrelevant to national security and to aggression. A more heavily populated country will only starve more quickly in all the foreseeable future.

In the minds of some people, however, the ability and willingness, or carelessness and irresponsibility, of producing large families is still regarded as somehow admirable. A change in that attitude is one of the acute needs of the world.

Perhaps the greatest need from science in the world now is the discovering or inventing of a simple, cheap, certain and harmless method of birth control, which could be used effectively even by ignorant and relatively irresponsible people to produce temporary sterility, or permanent sterility after they have had two or three children. Of course, if such a method were found by the scientists of one nation and advocated and distributed by the government or commercial enterprise of that nation, their motives might be open to biased interpretations as an attempt to weaken other peoples and enhance their own relative power. It would be foolish for any country to put itself in that position, but the same, or much better, research, education and promulgation could be undertaken without any such embarrassment by using those institutions set up for just such world purposes, the United Nations and its specialized agencies.

The constitutions of the appropriate agencies, the World Health Organization and the United Nations Educational, Scientific and Cultural Organization, provide for the undertaking of such research and educational work. The nations have only to direct those organizations to explore this problem of effective birth control without regard to expense to ensure that the best work that can be done in the world would be undertaken immediately. A few millions of dollars of such expenditure now could save many millions of lives, and probably riots, revolutions, much bloodshed and perhaps wars, in the near future.

Such action has not yet been taken because the politicians of too many countries are afraid to defy the taboo established by one sect of one religion. It is as simple as that. The World Health Assembly of 1952 showed a good example of that disastrous control over national and international policy. The delegate of Norway suggested setting up an expert committee to study the medical aspects of population problems. He was supported by a very few, at least one of them in knowing defiance of his own government's attitudes, but immediately the delegates from Belgium, Italy, France, Lebanon, Spain, Panama, Costa Rica and Ireland registered their immovable opposition, stating that they might be forced to withdraw from the World Health Organization if the Assembly decided to set up such a committee. Delegates from many other countries avoided any commitment and did everything possible to avoid a vote, as the most constructive thing they could do, not daring to vote for the Norwegian proposal. Delegates from the United States of America, United Kingdom, Canada and many others were in that position. The delegate from the United States of America put the situation very mildly when he stated "W.H.O. might lose much good will if we set up a population committee."

At this moment at least two thirds of the world's people are suffering from malnutrition. Neither food production in the world nor methods of distribution of food in the world are adequate to the needs of the world's population at the present time. Hopes have been expressed that by development of the resources of the oceans for growing food, by irrigation of deserts, and by many other new methods it may be possible to increase food production in the world very greatly. Still even when that may become possible there is no evidence at the present time that our methods of distribution will be able to keep up with the increase in production. Our economic and monetary systems are not designed for the purpose of feeding the peoples of the world.

It is commonly believed that with a rising standard of living the population increase is reduced considerably, but it is alarming to note that the present rate of increase per hundred thousand of population is greater in the United States of America than it is in India. The higher infant and general mortality rate in India is largely responsible for this difference, but it is to be expected that, with the rapidly increasing efficiency of health services in India, the survival rate there in the future will increase greatly.

We must remind ourselves repeatedly that a higher standard of living also requires very much more space per person in any population. Provision must be made for space for housing, for garages, for greatly increased road systems, for factories, for parks, for all the requirements of a highly developed culture which has acquired a high standard of living.

The peoples of the world are going to have to make a choice. They are going to have to decide whether they will continue to increase their population at or about the present rate or limit populations to the point where it will be possible for the peoples of the world to live comfortably, with room enough to enjoy their living.

Can the nations learn to face this great problem honestly and sensibly in time to prevent chaos? This is still to be seen, but it is clear that archaic taboos will have to be by-passed or trampled down first.

VII.

Natural Resources

AT THE present time North America is using approximately half of the world's production of natural resources, oil, coal, iron, aluminum, copper, tin, nickel and many others. It has been stated that, since the First World War, more of the world's irreplaceable natural resources have been used by North America than were used by the whole human race throughout all their history before that time.

There is now an increasing acceptance of the belief that peace and freedom from fear in the world can be found only when a roughly equal standard of living has been attained throughout the world. That seems to be a reasonable belief, but movement in that direction raises many tremendous problems.

Increasingly, the less economically developed countries will be reluctant to export anything but finished products, as their own rising standard of living will require retention of more and more of their own natural resources and raw material at home. They will also begin to think of conservation to safeguard their own future developments.

The ability of the United Kingdom to support its present population is based very largely on the import of raw materials, the export of finished products and the transportation involved. Increasingly the United States of America and other industrialized countries are dependent on raw materials from the less developed parts of the world, and on foreign markets for their manufactured goods.

What will be the situation when, in the near future, many more countries reach that same stage of industrialization? Why would Egypt sell raw cotton to other countries instead of raising its own standard of living by manufacturing its cotton at home and selling the finished product? Why would eastern Mediterranean, Asian and South American countries allow foreigners to exploit and profit greatly from their oil resources whenever they will have reached a stage of technical and social development at which they can do the job themselves? Why would Liberia continue to allow her rich, but limited, iron ore reserves to be used for the benefit of foreign steel industries and to support the already very high standard of living in some other country? Will not Liberia also process and manufacture itself all the rubber grown in its own territory?

These and many other countries will not long be content or willing to dissipate their irreplaceable assets, or to feed to their competitors raw materials they will need for their own development. They will not be greatly concerned to keep up standards of living in the countries already far ahead of their own.

Even if the pressing problem of disposal of radioactive waste products can be solved (and it is very far from solved yet), and atomic energy made available all over the world, that will not increase the supply or the reserves of raw material for the heavily industrialized countries with high standards of living. Indeed it may lead to every country freezing all export of natural resources and raw materials for use and development at home. Certainly it will end the present era of excessive shares for a small proportion of the world's people.

What are the nations doing to prepare for that probability of the near future? It would seem that from the point of view of the whole human race, a world government and the breaking down of the competitive nation system may be the only hope. This is particularly true for the highly industrialized countries, every one of which must import raw materials to support even its present population and anything like its present standard of living, and the populations of the highly industrialized countries are generally increasing rapidly.

These are areas in which the United Nations, properly used, could be most helpful. It is already late but much might still be done to ease the shock of the economic revolution which seems to be approaching rapidly.

The underdeveloped countries have nothing, or little, to lose, but the threat to the highly developed countries with high standards of living is very real and very serious. For them failure of the inflow of raw materials means, inevitably, drastic reductions in their standards of living. For a while the excessive population increases in many underdeveloped countries may force them to buy food from the industrialized countries, or from those of them which can produce an excess of foods. The United Kingdom will not be in that category, but the U.S.A., Canada, and a few others may be if their own populations have not by that time increased too much.

In countries with high living standards, housing, great estates, golf courses, flower gardens, parks, game preserves, sports fields, big industries, oil refineries and storage tanks, railways, airfields, four- and six-lane highways, service stations, schools, colleges and universities, water storage for hydroelectric power development, power lines, navigation canals, ever-increasing cemeteries and many other increasing users of space which might produce food may have to be curtailed drastically if population growth goes on as it is now and lack of world co-operation greatly reduces available supplies of raw materials.

No one country can do much about this developing problem. Governments, under the present system, must look after their own people first. Several governments recently have been accused by their people, or by opposition parties, of selling out their irreplaceable assets to foreigners, and many other governments are vulnerable to that same attack. There has been a headlong rush to exploit oil resources, for instance, as quickly as possible, even when 50 per cent or more of the profits go out of the country of origin. Of course, it would be far better for the people of such a country to develop their oil production much more slowly as they could modernize their own education and train their own people to do the work themselves, and retain all the profits. Their oil, or iron, or tin, or manganese would last much longer and their cultures could develop in much more orderly and consistent ways.

Unfortunately for many underdeveloped countries, control has been in the hands of a few dollar-hungry people who saw chances to profit greatly themselves and have done so with relatively little gain to the masses of their people. In some cases rulers have undertaken constructive work, irrigation, road building, housing and so on, but on the whole only a small proportion of total profits has gone back to the people whose birthright is being dissipated.

Gradually the people of the underdeveloped countries are coming to see that their true interest lies in educating themselves to undertake their own development, retaining their own natural resources and their own potentially enormous markets. They will still welcome foreign investment for some time yet, but increasingly will insist that such investments be self-liquidating and subject to expropriation whenever the government concerned is confident of the ability of its own people to carry on the development.

The consequences in the economies of the investing nations will be very great and possible ways of preventing such developments as these from seriously threatening the standard of living of the more developed countries will need to be evolved co-operatively. This is clearly an area where early study and effective action on a world basis are indicated. Until the most highly developed nations recognize how deeply their own prosperity is involved in this problem, the United Nations agencies particularly qualified to undertake the necessary study and planning are not able to take really effective steps. It is to be hoped that recognition will come soon enough to avoid very widespread economic disaster and misery. The World Bank for Reconstruction and Development, the International Monetary Fund, the Economic Commissions and the Economic and Social Council of the United Nations are the competent bodies to undertake the necessary planning, but it may be that such plans can be implemented effectively only after some sort of world government has been established.

The last great areas of the earth not already held by one or another nation for their own advantage are to be found in the Antarctic, and perhaps a little in the Arctic. Never in history have such rich prizes been grabbed peacefully; always claims have been settled by war or threats from positions of strength. What is to be done about the great potentialities of Antarctica will depend on the early enough development of some form of world federation to prevent war and to ensure an equitable distribution. Obviously most of the natural resources of Antarctica should go to the world's most needy people, particularly in Asia and Africa where most of them are.

VIII.

Language

ONE OF the frustrating world problems, brought into focus far more sharply now than ever before, is difficulty of communication across language barriers. The United Nations and its specialized agencies use five official languages and varying numbers of working languages.

However amazingly adept is the simultaneous translation at thousands of meetings held by international organizations, many misunderstandings creep in, antagonistic feelings are aroused or stimulated, enormous costs are incurred in interpretation of addresses and translations of thousands of documents, and reproducing them in several languages.

Educated people in most European, African, Asian, and South American countries normally speak at least one language well, and commonly several, besides their own. That ability is relatively rare among natively English- and French-speaking people, whose reluctance to learn and use other languages is often resented.

That there is a very real need for a common world language is obvious and insistent to those whose work or interests involve communication in several languages. Such a common medium of understanding will be essential in the future as world organization and co-operation become more efficient. Unfortunately, as in so many problems, national prestige is involved, which adds greatly to the difficulties of finding a solution.

Many suggestions have been made as to the best, or most generally acceptable, methods of overcoming this great handicap to world understanding. Esperanto and other "artificial" languages have been advocated widely and there is much to be said for adoption of one of these for all international communication. Not least among its advantages would be a reduction in oratory, local idiom, anecdote, literary allusion and other irrelevant material in addresses at international meetings. More conservative suggestions have been that all nations should introduce a second language in their school-teaching from early grades, and that this second language should be either English or French. Actually more countries speak Spanish as a native language than any other, though outside of Central and South America Spanish is little used for international communication. Whatever plan is eventually adopted by the nations will take at least forty or fifty years to implement effectively, so there is every reason for early study, decision and constructive action.

It would be appropriate for the nations of the world to ask Unesco, with the highest priority, to develop a plan for consideration by all national legislative bodies and discussion in the Economic and Social Council and the General Assembly of the United Nations, and Unesco might well be asked to assist governments in implementation, when a plan has been adopted. Because of concern for their national prestige by so many governments, it may be that no effective action can be taken on this pressing matter until nationalism has become less common and "world-mindedness" has spread much more widely, perhaps not even until some form of world federation or world government is established.

IX.

Money

SOONER or later, the people of the world will have to do something about the monetary chaos which now plagues business, governments, international organizations and traveling individuals. There is no apparent reason except tradition for having great numbers of different currencies. The costs in mistakes and time of such accidental systems as those of many countries are enormous.

People used to using a metric system, visiting a country with an irregular and irrational currency, resent their confusion and inability to appreciate prices or to know whether they are given correct change when they make purchases. The unnecessary complications of bookkeeping, whether done by hand or machine, are a heavy burden on the economy of such a country. The necessity to translate prices into other currencies is time and paper consuming, with no compensating advantages. The United Kingdom and other countries using sterling are good examples of this type of self-handicapping.

Of course, one standard currency for the world is the only sensible and eventually the only possible solution, but prejudices and the cost of the change postpone such rational action, and probably it will be many years before that can be accomplished.

The preparation of a plan for a world currency might well be entrusted by the nations to the International Bank for Reconstruction and Development and the International Monetary Fund, both specialized agencies of the United Nations; but probably not until after some form of world government, also inevitable, is established can sensible reform be carried out in this most conservative, or backward, of fields. Of course, there are many complications to be considered and, as usual, national prestige is involved, but delay will not make the solution easier, and the present situation is manifestly absurd.

X.

Race

WHILE pressure of population is relatively new as a world problem, that of racial prejudice is very ancient. Color of skin has been accepted commonly as in itself, and not just indicative of, a superiority or inferiority. One must be very short of evidence against one's own feeling of inferiority to have to rely on skin color for a feeling of superiority. Of course, to any intelligent and unprejudiced person, skin color has no meaning except the accident of heredity. Just as intelligent, just as noble, or generous, or mature, or wise or "good" people have existed, and do exist, in all colors the members of the human race are capable of assuming. Still the prejudice dies hard; in spite of its ridiculousness, it still complicates the lives of large numbers of people in large areas of the world. Of course, the basic cause is human cupidity and the long-encouraged ability of the human to fool himself, whenever it is to his material or emotional advantage to do so. Many people, otherwise relatively civilized, have been able to find excuses for enslaving or exploiting individuals or groups of an alien color in the old chronicles and folk tales of ancient tribes. This reference back to early and primitive tribal attitudes is now found almost exclusively among Christians and is the last stronghold of barbarism and prejudice in the very important areas of relations between color groups.

Careful investigations have brought any assurance that was necessary, for those who are timid about violation of old local taboos and prejudices about race, that there are no inherent "superiorities" or "inferiorities" in this or that group distinguishable by color.

Laws against miscegenation, recognized as absurd by unprejudiced people, are oppressive encroachments on human liberty, and have no proper place in the statutes of mature states.

Segregation of colored and white people is now practiced with legal protections in only a few of the backward areas of the world. South Africa, the Belgian Congo, but less so recently, and parts of the southern parts of the United States of America are the worst offenders against rational behavior in this area of rabid prejudice, though many millions in other places show the same prejudice in less active forms. Where such prejudices direct or influence government policy, revolution is not only inevitable sooner or later, but, in the minds of many people, is justified.

The United Nations, throughout the few years of its life, has been trying to soften this particular prejudice, and some progress is being made; but the nations, or some of them, have a long way to go before all prejudice on account of color of skin has disappeared.

The Nazi doctrine of a superior race, long proven completely fallacious, has relatively few adherents now. Manifestations of the same attitudes still exist but, though they make local difficulties and sometimes serious ones, none of them is a world problem. The absurdities of claims to inherited superiority because one's ancestors belonged to a particular Scottish clan, or crossed the Atlantic in a particular ship at a particular time, or were rewarded for financial, political, amorous or other services by a title, or were part of a particular revolution, or announced themselves to be "God's Chosen People," are now evident to almost everyone, except to those unfortunates who still need to use such claims to bolster their poverty-stricken egos.

It is in relation to the necessary movement toward world federation, for the security or perhaps even the survival of the people of the world, that racial discrimination is a very important barrier. It is one of the irrational prejudices that tends to slow rational social development. If it persists too long the colored people of the world may well feel justified in assuming a domination over the white people, which could be possible in the not distant future. The whites form a minority of the race.

XI.

Freedom to Think

SINCE the early social development of man, two opposing orientations have appeared in his relations with both his real and his imagined environment.

The more basic, primitive and "natural" of these relationships was, and is, toward the security to be found in identification with nature, in the soil, the home, the native place, the love and protection of the mother, and in all the symbols which represent those types of security. That orientation showed long ago in matriarchal societies, the close-knit family or clan, to which all nonmembers were outlanders and enemies, but all members were potentially equal, and in the protective ancient goddesses. More recently the same urges find expression in nationalism, "momism," Mariolatry, patriotism, racism, all kinds of exclusive "loves" and loyalties, and also in reactions against reason, world-mindedness, United Nations, "internationalism," dynamic psychology, miscegenation and all the other extensions of love beyond the family or tribe or other limited group.

The other orientation has been, and is, toward the development of reason, wide social relationships, personal responsibility, pursuit of knowledge, and showed in the past in the patriarchal societies, "father gods," tribal laws, commerce, study and research, exploration, etc. Such attitudes now find their expression in "free thought," reason, world-mindedness, refusal to accept the old hierarchical controls or orthodox explanations of previous generations; in general a looking forward instead of backward for authority and a "belonging" feeling with the whole human race, and not just a part of it.

Of all the less socially valuable manifestations still persisting of the ancient attitudes, nationalism and exclusive patriotism are probably the most dangerous.

In June, 1937, the late Dr. H. G. Baynes, speaking to the Analytical Psychology Club in England, made a statement to the effect that the whole future of civilization depends on one single eventuality, namely, whether the conception of sovereign states is to be absolute. If they refuse in the last resort to submit their national claims to a supranational tribunal, then it means the collapse of civilization. But if the approach of suicide quickens a response that can shake the civilized world to its foundations, it is possible that the idea of a supranational symbol of authority, which all must obey, will bind the nations together, not from choice, but from necessity.

Nationalism and exclusive patriotism are incompatible with the only real hope of peace in the world or indeed with the survival of the human race. They make the welfare of a part of the race appear to be more important than that of the whole, which is ridiculous, unless the untenable concept of "superiority" of some part of the race is held against all evidence. Unfortunately, in the minds of the people who hold such attitudes, faith, tradition, limited loyalties, childhood teachings, religious authority, are all given preference over evidence.

To such persons any attempt to study history in the light of new insights, or to adjust any of the early learned patterns of belief to newly recognized realities, is decried as "heresy" or "iconoclasm," as indeed it is. In fact, it is only through such processes of heresy and iconoclasm that any progress has been made toward developing man's freedom to be rational, and to think and act appropriately to his real situation. Every step in the direction of real world solidarity, not dominated by any one religion, orthodoxy or hierarchy, has been and is still being fought bitterly by the orthodox.

The Buddha is reported to have said: "Believe nothing, no matter where you read it or who has said it, not even if I have said it, unless it agrees with your own reason and your own common sense." The attitude is not new.

A quotation from George Bernard Shaw's *Major Barbara* is very apt. "Well, you have made for yourself something that you call a morality or a religion or whatnot. It doesn't fit the facts. Well scrap it. Scrap it and get one that does fit. That is what is wrong with the world at present. It scraps its obsolete steam engines and dynamos; but it won't scrap its old prejudices and its old moralities and its old religions and its old political constitutions. What's the result? In machinery it does very well; but in morals and religion and politics it is working at a loss which brings it nearer bankruptcy every year. Don't persist in that folly!"

It is encouraging, however, to see that in all countries there are many individuals and groups of people, indigenous growths, who increasingly are throwing off the shackles of traditionally imposed limited loyalties. They are beginning to feel themselves citizens of the world, and are developing a wider interest and responsibilities that go with that more mature status. Such people are the best, perhaps the only real, hope of the world.

They should be distinguished clearly from the people who, while interested on a world scale and often sincerely devoted, are working in the interests of an "ideology" or a particular religion or hierarchy. Some of these devoted but misguided people still continue to proclaim an ancient type of anthropomorphic god, so far out of date that his attitudes and advertised behavior would not be acceptable, or even legally allowable, in any culture of this generation. Unfortunately, some sincere missionaries still carry these uncivilized ideals to many ignorant people, still teaching for instance, that their ideal god takes vengeance on innocent people to the third and fourth generation for the sins of long-dead ancestors, and that all manner of tortures await, in a life after death, those who persist in thinking for themselves in this world.

Is it not reasonable that many governments of the less-developed countries are anxious to get rid of such confused and confusing people, when those governments are trying to move toward rationality and justice?

For far too long the young people, the people whose thinking processes have not been crippled by early imposed controls, and those who have fought themselves free of morbid fears of hell-fire and damnation and of disapproval of the elders, have hesitated to proclaim their freedom to develop. Social pressures, economic pressures (because a "free thinker" could not keep his job in many cultures or subcultures), modesty in the face of overwhelming public opinion and inculcated respect for the elders, whether worthy of respect or not, have all combined to beat down the nonconformers.

Even now that physical torture can rarely be used to defend the orthodoxies, more subtle forms of controls can still be very effective. The enormous cumulative effect on the development of children of the words "What will your father (or Mrs. Jones, or the minister, or God) think if you behave like that?" is rarely appreciated. These, or words like them, are commonly used to control any attempt to behave experimentally or independently, and particularly any disobedience. Someone else's "thinking" is presented to the child as a dread process of which even the all-powerful mother is afraid. Such words greatly reinforce the strength of the controls exercised by public opinion, and particularly orthodox public opinion, against the innovator, or independent thinker, and tend to prevent rational development, such as population control, world federation, or other necessary changes.

With the best of intentions many parents use such methods to enforce obedience to parental ideals, faiths or even conveniences. Enforcement by use of a stick or strap or fist, though also not at all helpful to the child's rational progress, might well be less damaging to the future development and social value of the child.

The ultimate degree of such damage is produced by the concept of the "all-seeing, all-hearing God," who knows even what children are thinking and will disapprove and punish for secret behavior and for "wicked" or "evil" thoughts, which are just anything the child thinks the mother would not like. But this vicious concept is such a useful instrument for enforcing either reasonable or unreasonable controls on the small child that sincere people who earnestly believe in the "goodness" of obedience, conformity, purity (meaning absence of interest in sex), but who are without psychological insight, cannot be expected to give it up.

Most tragically this concept imposes a strong taboo on intellectual experimentation and pioneering. It is this type of magic control which is the strongest barrier to the development of a free imagination, and a free imagination is very important for successful development toward maturity.

For many centuries man's imagination has been both his hope and his despair, depending on whether it was used rationally or irrationally. It was early man's imagination which stimulated and guided him in experiments with fire and with water, with sharp tools, with stabbing and cutting weapons, with the lever and the wedge, and, much later, the wheel. The same function of imagination is still basic to all scientific development. It is imagination which has rescued man, to a greater extent than any of the other forms of life on this planet, from dependence on the local environment and from development by chance. Imagination provides an opportunity for man effectively to take charge of his own destiny—an opportunity far from realized up to this time.

Unfortunately, while throughout all these thousands of years some men have been earnestly using imagination for sound exploration of whatever parts of the total environment could be got at, others have been perverting that same supreme function in the interests of their own power, or prestige. These distorters of reality have used their imaginations to people all the unknown or ununderstood parts of their environment with spirits and hobgoblins and ghosts and werewolves and gods and saints and devils and fairies and jinn and innumerable other fanciful creatures. Some are supposed to be feared and avoided or propitiated, some to be worshiped and some both feared and worshiped.

The most diverse and bizarre patterns of reward and punishment have been projected into an "afterlife." Always the rewards are for the people who throughout their earthly life are obedient in thought and behavior to the rules imposed by the dominant hierarchy. The minor punishments are for aggressive behavior against fellow men, but the really savage punishments are reserved for those daring to question the absolute authority of the mystic hierarchy.

Matthew puts it very clearly in the Christian Bible (12:31, 32): "but whosoever speaketh against the Holy Ghost, it shall not be forgiven him, neither in this world, neither in the world to come."

In various systems of faith the delights and terrors of these illusory places, invented by morbid imaginations, have been used to bribe and frighten hundreds of millions of people into obedience and, most importantly, into that thought-controlled state where they dare not think independently. These, particularly the devils, hells, punishing gods, demons and so on, are the guardians of the concept of "sin," without which they, and their earthly representatives, would be powerless.

The only thing all these figments of the imagination have in common is irrationality and their value to some person or persons for the purpose of controlling someone else. Yet these poisonous fruits of man's imagination have in all known times and places enslaved men's minds and bodies in the service of the power of some person or group.

Almost always these potent forces have supported special interests, controlled by a person or group; they have fought bitterly and ruthlessly against extension of knowledge, because always such extensions of knowledge weakened the faith in their magic explanations and it was on their magic that their power and thought control depended and still depends.

All over the world, while some frightened people rush back to orthodoxy and obedience, others often no less frightened, but reacting rationally and in increasing numbers to their real fears, are beginning to look at man, and themselves, in objective ways, earnestly trying to divest themselves of the crippling faiths which they learned in infancy.

There should be no objection to anyone teaching anything, or crying any belief he has from the housetops, or on the radio or television, as long as children are not exposed to exclusive faiths, which label all doubt or disagreement or even contrary scientific evidence as "sin" or "heresy."

If children's minds can be protected from certainty of "rightness" of any one ideological, religious, educational, social, economic or other experiment, and consequent "wrongness" of all other experiments, they will be far more likely to be able to react rationally, that is, sensibly, to the dreadful problems the coming generations will meet.

Of course, the hierarchies supporting all certainties, orthodoxies, dogmas, and rigid ideologies and loyalties know that only by imposing their rules on children before the critical functions of their intellects have developed can thought control be established and maintained.

Many intelligent, thoughtful and socially responsible parents are now recognizing that a major part of their obligation to their own children, and to the next generation as a whole, is to protect them from such sectional certainties, so that during their progress toward maturity they may be free to do their own thinking, and choose their own experiments. Surely no parent should feel justified in teaching a child some belief as true, simply because of the accident of the time and place of his own birth. To leave a child's thinking and imagination free is to give him the greatest possible endowment, by virtue of which he may reach a far higher level of maturity than his parents have been able to attain.

Imagination has been defined in many ways according to the likes and dislikes of the definer. It may be more useful to try to describe some of the normal functions of imagination and their values and give some consideration to the preservation of those functions and avoidance of their paralysis or distortion.

Perhaps foremost in importance among these functions is that of exploration. The sort of questions an active, free and well-developed imagination will answer truly are, "What will happen if I do so and so?" "What will be the result if I go to such and such a place?" "What will be the effect if I say this or that?" "Will those happenings, results or effects be desirable for me? For others? For my relationship with myself and with others?" "Will they enhance or outweigh and diminish whatever satisfactions I may expect my actions to produce? Over a short period? Over a long period?" "Taking all expected satisfactions, effects and side effects, on myself and everyone else, into account, is this projected action desirable or not?" "What possible changes in circumstances might make it more or less desirable?" Finally, "Shall I do, go or say, or not?"

A well-developed imagination goes through such a sequence as this, dealing efficiently with very many variables, with a speed and accuracy favorably comparable with the work of an electric calculator. In a free mind, its adjustability to fit changing circumstances is far more rapid and efficient than that of the calculator, and it can deal with shifting, not only with fixed or predetermined or mathematically measurable, values. In order to be able to perform this extremely valuable both individually and socially protective and constructive function, imagination needs a favorable soil and climate and freedom to develop. It is not a plant that can be pruned or tied into bizarre shapes without destroying its functioning. To use a military analogy, we may see this particular function of imagination as a combined strategic intelligence and spy service and tactical scouting service, but invisible and immune to capture. This can be a marvelous instrument with which to assure effective action, but almost universally it is destroyed, distorted or its development grossly limited by the imposition of control in the form of prejudices, taboos and guilts in childhood. The "evil thoughts" of the confessional are examples of such guilt-making taboos, and destroyers of the imagination's exploratory and preparatory function in biological development. In reality, and until contaminated and spoiled by the dirty minds of the elders, these are beautiful, delightful and necessary explorations toward full, satisfying and effective life.

Without these early explorations normal sexual development is difficult or perhaps impossible to attain, and without that development the total personality will be distorted, life never more than partially experienced, and excessive pressures will develop toward inappropriate substitute goals.

Not only in the sexual field is this exploratory function of imagination crippled. If a book, a doctrine, a constitution, a social or economic system, a person or anything else is made unquestionably right or sacred or wrong and taboo in childhood, the contemporary validity of those judgments may not be questioned without guilt and anxiety; imagination is forbidden within the taboo area. Conscience stands guard, armed with the weapons of accusation of disloyalty, sin and guilt, against any attempt to understand, to consider evidence or to revise appropriately to changed circumstances.

Because it is very clear that many established rites, taboos and sacrednesses are no longer applicable in our present world, and often act as an impenetrable barrier between ourselves and others, this type of crippling of imagination must be recognized as dangerous to our social progress and indeed to our very existence.

There is a common belief that children must have certainties, areas of absolute belief, and it does appear that in one field such certainty tends to an important degree to facilitate development toward maturity. In emotional relationship with parents perfect confidence is of very great benefit. To know that one is loved for oneself, uncritically and independently of one's behavior, is of major importance in the early stages of personality development. Lack of love, loss of love or fear of such loss are principal sources of anxiety. That need is generally recognized, but, given confidence in that one area of basic importance, it would seem the child does not need any other certainties or any answers in absolute terms. It is in the presence of an already established anxiety that uncertainties are felt to be threatening. Taboos which may not be questioned, protected by parental disapproval, tend to destroy that basis of confidence in parents from which the unknown is not fearful but stimulating, not anxiety-making but productive of interest and wonder and welcome challenge. The certain parent tends to produce the anxious child, who then protectively adopts certainties and tends to repeat the process with his own children. And so faiths are propagated and development of reason and reasonable solutions of world problems is delayed.

Every child finds that local customs impose certain restrictions on his behavior, according to the accident of time, place and parentage into which he happens to have been born. Human behavior can be trained into great varieties of patterns, given sufficient ruthlessness on the part of the trainers. Because the rightness of local customs is taken for granted by most parents, no trouble on their part and no pain to the child are thought to be too great if they can assure firm establishment of the locally acceptable patterns of conformity on the part of the child. Of course, a sufficient degree of conformity to local customs is essential to peaceful living in groups of human beings, but that degree, sufficient for the requirements of the laws of the group, often is not enough to bring credit to the parents. Rarely, if ever, do young children have primary difficulty in fitting their behavior to the legal requirements of their time and place.

As long as the necessity for conformity to the local customs is confined to the field of overt behavior, few children are handicapped seriously in their emotional development. Imagination, if free, is well able to take care of many natural urges and reactions to external control which are not allowed outlet in frank behavior. Outlet given to pressures and desires through imagination is not as satisfying as is complete release in behavior, but neither does it have any of the uncomfortable, dangerous or even disastrous consequences that may follow real behavior which is not approved by the particular culture.

This is the second major function of the imagination, that of "safety valve." A healthy, free imagination can be used to escape temporarily from the local limitations placed on behavior. That escape can be long enough to provide enough satisfaction for a particular emotional urge so that it will not have to be "repressed," pushed down into the unconscious, where it would be a disrupting force. An illustration may be useful.

If a child, or anyone else, is treated in a way he thinks is unfair, is bullied by a stronger person or by some authority, is taken advantage of in any way, his normal feeling is one of resentment and antagonism. That feeling calls for aggressive action against the offender, primarily physical action, but in most circumstances in most cultures immediate physical retaliation would make worse trouble.

Laws, public opinion, keeping one's job, all sorts of realities, must be considered and such consideration leads to the conclusion that physical retaliation cannot be allowed. Imagination, however, can perform much of the same function as action, without trouble with the laws or public opinion or risk of unemployment. The healthy imagining of assaulting the offender as thoroughly as one would like to, beating him into as bloody a pulp as one's natural urges would desire, gives a considerable amount of satisfaction. An active and free imagination will go on from there and recognize that disposal of the body represents a difficult problem, with risk of imprisonment or execution, and that to satisfy the urge in reality would be a great mistake. However, the feeling has already been satisfied to some extent, the tension reduced and "tension symptoms" such as high blood pressure, pain in the back, gastric ulcers, "nervous heart," "nervous indigestion" or any other of the long chain of possible psychosomatic symptoms will not be needed, unless feelings of guilt have been produced.

Again if a healthy young, or not so young, male sees an attractive young, or not so young, female, a rousing of the sexual urge is quite usual. In a state of nature the natural reaction would be to drag her off to his lair, but, by common agreement, that is not allowed in most places now. The natural next best healthy substitute is to be found in imagination. Refusal to recognize and accept the fact of sexual pressure eventually leads also to any of a great variety of mental and physical symptoms, and loss of ability to live satisfactorily.

These functions of imagination are very valuable and necessary to the establishment and maintenance of desirable cultural controls of behavior. They are harmless unless they produce guilt, and conviction of sin, but that happens only when children are misled and frightened about the entirely fictitious damaging consequences of such uses of imagination. All healthy people do it anyway, but in the process many assume really serious loads of guilt, sin and anxiety, and the consequent crippling, personal and social, that they produce. It is the concept of sin that makes all the trouble, not the entirely normal use of imagination.

It is this function of imagination which protects our ability to be civilized, that is, to behave in the ways prescribed by the local culture. The damage is caused by attempts to carry civilized attitudes too deeply into the personality. We shall be very content if behavior can be civilized satisfactorily; attempts to go deeper are not successful and defeat their own purpose by producing physical or mental or social symptoms, such as juvenile delinquency, or criminality, homosexuality or any of many other unwanted patterns of behavior.

Much fear has been expressed by proponents of the old systems of thought and behavior controls that without those systems behavior would be uncontrolled and civilization would break down. Actually there is no reliable evidence supporting that fear. Conscious self-control seems to do a much better job than external control through fear of the supernatural or of public opinion.

There are now in many places many responsible and useful citizens who were brought up from infancy without any fears of supernatural interference in human affairs, or of punishment in a future life or hope of personal reward. One of the methods used commonly in the tactical defense of the hierarchical interests is the accusation of lack of ethics outside the particular system being defended. In fact a very high proportion of the most valuable people devoting their lives to the welfare of all people everywhere are quite independent of any such systems of thought control, and privately voice their concern about the harm to emotional-social development that imposition of one-sided attitudes does to children all over the world. Some of them, however, lacking courage, or appreciation of the degree of damage, and because of pressure of lagging public opinion, still allow their own children to be taught exclusive national and religious loyalties.

XII.

Pathological Reactions

IN ALL humans who find themselves frustrated, insecure, anxious, bewildered, frightened, persecuted or in any circumstances with which they cannot cope effectively from the point of view of their own security or welfare, there is a tendency to regress, to retreat to less mature, more childlike or more primitive behavior. This same tendency can be seen in cultures also.

The less mature the individual, the easier is this regressive shift in the face of difficulties, and this also seems to be true of cultures. Many aspects of the present world situation are potent and valid causes for such feelings of insecurity, anxiety, frustration, bewilderment, etc., and it must be accepted as inevitable that less mature people, and cultures, will show signs of these regressive tendencies.

Among really primitive peoples, of course, and among those not well developed socially, depending still on orthodoxies and hierarchies or absolute hereditary rules or dictators for their control, only very slight disturbances of security, even of prestige status, can be enough to produce overthrow of governments, revolutions, mob violence, assassinations and other primitive reactions. In more developed groups such disturbing feelings as those suggested above may result in less mob reaction, but more signs of individual regression. These may be seen in tendencies to return to old obsolete types of social adjustment, or even quite unsocial escapes, such as alcoholism. Hero worship, aggrandizements of "leaders," suspicion of strangers or foreigners; demands for conformity, particularly to parental or earlier types of behavior and even of thinking, resulting in "witch-hunting," a sort of "scapegoat" pattern; retreat to more emotional

82

and less intellectual religious patterns, "revivals"; retreat from intellectual judgment to "faiths," astrology, magic; great concern for "security" rather than appropriate progress and change; acute nationalism; racism—these and many such phenomena can be seen at the present time.

Typical of this regression is the demand that everyone be labeled "for us or against us," that everyone must "take sides," "stand up and be counted," discard reservations, be a "hundred-percenter" or answer "yes" or "no" to all questions, all of which the educated, mature person can rarely do. The hundred-percenters see that inability as a threatening weakness and call such a person names like "egg-head" or "intellectual," which apparently mean a person who has, and uses, brains.

A related pattern of regression may show a childlike tendency to defy and rebel against any controls, particularly against any expectation of self-control, and may be seen in searches for more and more defiant patterns in music, painting, sculpture, sex relations, clothing, manners or almost anywhere else.

All these reactions distract attention from the real problems of the world. These are serious symptoms of pathological reactions to ununderstood threats, but they are not themselves the real problems. They can, however, be very effective barriers against serious study and against implementation of any rational plan to deal with the real problems.

It is not easy for the people whose reactions continue in more firmly established mature patterns to deal effectively with such widespread mental illness as is now affecting much of mankind. That illness establishes hectic political atmospheres, climates of excitable public opinion, storms of popular condemnation or worship, and tends to label appeals to fact-finding and rational approach heretical, disloyal, iconoclastic, subversive or what not. Any attempt to whip up counteremotion against all this regression can only attract the unstable, looking for a new magic, the starry-eyed, the egotistical searchers for martyrdom, the parlor intellectuals, the rebels or others who are undesirable as supporters of a rational course of action. It seems to remain then for the mature to write only for the mature, or the nearly mature; but while that is probably true of writing, it may be that effective and stimulating communication with the somewhat less mature may be established through the spoken rather than the written word. Particularly that may be so if the approach is made at certain periods of life history.

The intelligent postadolescent, not yet resigned to the humbug and cynicism or the gushing emotionalism of his seniors, is often looking for reason and organized thinking, which is at the same time free to experiment and is not rigid. He sometimes hopes to find it in an authoritarian religion or in a religio-social doctrine such as Communism, but that is to buy a temporary peace of mind at the excessive price of intellectual integrity, and fortunately relatively few are willing finally to pay that price, though many hopefully try these escapes.

The young parent, or soon-to-be parent, is sometimes seriously concerned about the state of the world into which the child is to be introduced and would like to be able to think constructively about world problems.

Young teachers, and some elderly ones, impressed with their responsibilities, and not yet casual or calloused, very often know they want help.

Speakers to, or leaders of, discussions with groups of such people can often convey encouragement, help to strengthen the desire to think logically, and assist further development in the direction of maturity, and do it much more effectively than in writing. The personal contact, the opportunity for question and discussion, the voicing of doubts or objections, all facilitate rational communication.

Of course, the best time at which to acquire basic knowledge of human nature and the habit of rational thinking is in early childhood, but there are still great difficulties facing anyone who would suggest that children should be taught human dynamic psychology beginning in their earliest school years and continuing throughout their time at school. The real objection would be on the part of parents and teachers who would not like to have young children recognizing childish, even infantile, behavior in their elders. How could Father have a temper tantrum with any pleasure with Junior taking notes for discussion in his psychology group? How could Mother throw a satisfactory hysterical fit under little Mary's coldly scientific eye? It might even be difficult for Father to vote for an ignorant or crooked political candidate if Junior were showing an interest in and insight into his real, in contrast to his expressed, motives. Such subversion in the home will not be allowed easily, but until it comes our social progress will not be very satisfactory.

There are some intelligent people who have reached, by long, slow and painful intellectual processes, convictions on social, political and personal matters which seem, and often are, valid and on a high level of social maturity. Such persons may be very valuable members of the world community, tolerant, kindly and helpful, and yet feel dissatisfied, unfulfilled, anxious, needing some closer, more personal protection and support. It may be that they have reached a high level of intellectual maturity, but lag behind emotionally. They find themselves needing personal reassurance and support, but cannot accept the older ideas of a sort of tribal, personal, manlike god, nor settle for anything less than a god of the universe. In such persons a faith has to be established, though often lost and regained many times, in a loving, fatherly, personally kindly, protective god of the universe, a very difficult concept but often reinforced by personal religious experience analogous to the "acceptance" reported by Roman Catholic nuns during and after their training period.

Because such persons do not deal in fear, overt threats of hell-fire, or miracles, their effect on developing children may often be far less socially damaging than that of the authoritarians, but they usually do implant the concept of the watchful, all-seeing god and the sinfulness of natural urges and so-called evil thoughts. These concepts produce feelings of personal guilt and inferiority which inevitably complicate the progress toward emotional maturity.

XIII.

Faith and Knowledge

IN ANY country whose people have been under the control of an orthodoxy, a recognition of the failures of that orthodox system, or of the social system supported by it, to deal effectively with poverty, misery and individual helplessness and hopelessness will be followed sooner or later by some form of revolution, which is reasonable and desirable. No social system which keeps any part of its people suppressed should command respect or support, nor should any faiths which support such a system.

Unfortunately the conditioned reaction of those people will be toward some other form of orthodoxy, which will provide competing but more hopeful absolutes. True liberal thinking does not develop that way, but is a slow growth in the minds of people who have been freed by their parents, or have been able themselves to fight free of dependence on dogma, hierarchies or totalitarianism.

Basically the "liberal" is a person whose beliefs must be acceptable to his intellect, and must be changeable as his knowledge and intellect develop. It is this demand for integrity of the whole personality, without any split between faith and intellect, which makes him a whole man, and allows development of all the potentials of his personality. Other factors may slow or prevent that full development, but at least he has gained freedom to think and to experiment.

It has been the fate, and at least partial defeat, of most liberal movements that seekers for a new faith have attached themselves, hailed such progressive attempts as discoveries of a new "religion," and rigidified and frozen them into new, or modifications of old, orthodoxies. It is not nearly so much the content of any orthodoxy which is destructive to the progress of man toward his full development as it is the fact of orthodoxy. Man does not need new and more certain or more promising faiths, but greater freedom from faiths, so that he may learn to define and develop his hopes. Of course, one may say that to do that one must have faith in the ability and capacity of man to affect his own development, but I think that is not true. He need only have the courage to think freely, to experiment and to learn from his experience. There is plenty of evidence that man is capable of doing that; many men have proven it. Belief in that capacity is justified by good objective evidence; no "faith" is necessary.

Much confusion is caused by the use of the terms "faith" and "belief" as though they were synonymous.[1] Discussion would be much clarified if the word "faith" were used only to indicate a firmly held certainty, independent of evidence or proof, reached by early imposition or emotional conviction, resting on other values than intellect and not changeable to adjust to new knowledge.

If that definition, or something like it, is not acceptable, then we need some other word for that kind of certainty which is not amenable to rational discussion or evidence. Or if "faith" and "belief" are to be used only to indicate somewhat different degrees of the same thing, with only a somewhat stronger connotation carried by "faith," then we need some other word for the "belief" of the scientist or that of any free mind.

For them belief is tentative, changeable as knowledge grows, results from a rational process of consideration of evidence, and is not applicable to the totally unknown. Perhaps most significantly the free mind does not fear the unknown, and is quite content to accept the fact that much remains unknowable at this stage of human development.

Speculation about the unknowns may be highly constructive, but any belief should await acceptable evidence. The great necessity in this generation is to try to catch up in practice with what knowledge is already available.

We know, for instance, that love is the only really socially con-

[1] Cf. Paul Tillich, *Dynamics of Faith: Faith and Belief, What They Are and What They Are Not,* World Perspectives, Vol. X.

structive human motivation, yet we teach our children our own patterns of prejudice, intolerance and hate. We know that our nationalistic attitudes are out of date and socially destructive, yet we teach our children our own narrow national loyalties.

We know that color of skin has no correlation with intelligence, with nobility of character or social value, yet most of the pinkish, so-called white people persist in their completely unreasonable prejudices against marriages between themselves and those with more brown, or black, or copper, or yellowish pigment in their skins.

Of course, what is really frightening to whites about the colored peoples is their own repressed guilt and shame for the savage ways in which they have treated them for so many generations. These attitudes about color of skin are found mostly among so-called Christians, but fortunately among only those of them whose faiths are really founded on old Hebrew customs, not on any attitudes of Jesus. There is no record of His showing any such absurd prejudices.

We know that while poverty does produce misery and a dangerous state of desperation, wealth does not necessarily produce happiness; yet many of us spend our whole lives in quite unconstructive work, just to accumulate more dollars than we need. We know that competitive national armament building is obsolete and dangerous to the whole race, and yet we go on multiplying national armaments, instead of vesting the police function of the world in a common pool that would be a threat to nobody.

The implications of all these and countless other lags in all our cultures can be avoided by retreat into mysticism, or patriotism, or some panacea that will avoid the unpleasant necessity of facing facts and of paying whatever may be necessary in the difficult coin of change in our own attitudes.

Harsh reality can never again be covered up by the soothing music of the cathedral organ, or responsibility avoided by the pious words of resignation which for so long have protected special interest: "God moves in a mysterious way His wonders to perform." It is man, not any god, who has enslaved or exploited his fellow man, who has built great wealth and prosperity on great misery and despair, and he is still doing it in the cathedral as well as in the palace.

In religious or national causes, which at this time exemplify human aspirations, there is little to inspire the devotion and selfless interest which man feels to be essential to his highest and most satisfying living. Marxism, in spite of Marx's many mistaken generalizations, does offer to its converts something of pioneering fervor, of identification with a great and idealistic cause, and opportunities for self-sacrifice in the interests of what they believe is the welfare of all mankind. Even a tangible enemy, a great asset to any cause, is presented in "capitalist imperialists."

The spirit of the convinced Marxist is reminiscent of that of the English, in their expansive and aggressive phase of development, while conquering as many as possible of the world's weaker peoples in the name of their empire, their commerce, and their God. This is the same spirit in which the North American Indians were slaughtered by whites, Spanish, Portuguese, French, British and American, all of whom were apparently convinced that they were behaving in highly virtuous ways.

In recent years large numbers of people have become more mature, more discriminative, and less able to find deep satisfactions in devotion to the aggrandizement of one nation, one religious group, one color group or indeed of any particular limited group of humans at the expense of others. It is the very catholicity of Marxism which makes it possible for many misguided people to swallow it, fallacies, ruthlessness, dogmas and all. At least it is advertised as, and believed by its faithful to be, for the good of all the world's masses of people, excluding, like other faiths, only those who willfully refuse to see the light, and fallacies, ruthlessness, dogmas and exclusions have been found in all their previous faiths.

Marxism, to many of those who live by faith and not by reason, can provide all, or almost all, the requirements of a satisfying religion; perhaps it answers more of the deep emotional human needs than does any of the other orthodoxies at this stage of their development. Of course its actual practice, as exemplified in communism, has proved shocking and bitterly disappointing to many immature hopeful people who felt that they had found the best of all faiths, but so also has the actual practice of the other orthodoxies.

Only gradually is the conviction coming to many people that what they are looking for, and deeply need, is not to be found in new and better faiths or return to old ones, unless the previously accepted meaning of the word "faith" is changed greatly.

Radhakrishnan in his *Recovery of Faith* [2] makes "faith" independent of dogmas, priestly authority or hierarchies, scriptural interpretations of history or of present reality or hereafter. Retained only is a belief in "the one God of all mankind who is worshiped in many ways," and the existence of a "soul," and the love of man. This may be seen as a redefinition of the word "faith," or a statement of what type of belief would be best for man, but it is not what the word has commonly meant until now.

This raises again an unsolved problem. With advanced knowledge and insight, of which incidentally Radhakrishnan shows both, should old-established words be enlarged or new words be used? An attempt to use old words to express new meanings can cause much misunderstanding. Some people will adopt the new and some will continue to use the old meaning, and the confused will do both, and add to the confusion.

Quite seriously, a system of symbols indicating just what meaning of any particular word is intended might be very useful. For instance faith (SR) for Sarvepalli Radhakrishnan, faith (RC) for Roman Catholic, faith (Mo) for Moslem, faith (H) for Hindu, faith (CUSA) for Constitution of the United States of America, faith (AWL) for American Way of Life (quite different from CUSA), faith (Com) for the Communist expression of faith, faith (Ma) for Marx, faith (Astro) for Astrology, all represent not just different content of faith but, in many cases, real differences in quality. Hundreds more could be listed, and all indicate a belief to some extent independent of evidence. They can be called faiths because, and I think only because, they have that one thing in common, a degree, greater or less, of independence of evidence. Discussions would be clarified if some such symbols could be attached to many words in common use, so everyone would know whose meaning is being used.

All this is no argument against, or for, the validity of Radhakrishnan's formulations, only that his title is, for many people, misleading, though there is still enough of the old meaning retained in his use of the word "faith" to make the title valid.

[2] World Perspectives, Vol. IV.

Again, in this discussion the word "evidence" needs some consideration. Many people believe that the mystical experience of relationship with God, reported by so many earnest seekers, is of itself conclusive evidence, not only for the existence of God, but also that he is the kind of God that they happen to believe in. These experiences are common in various states of mental-emotional disturbance, such as extended and deep conviction of sin, or in a state of illness or starvation, or under hypnosis or anesthetic.

For scientifically oriented observers, psychological or psychopathological explanations are easier, and seem to fit the facts better. The psychologist does not, of course, argue against the reality of these experiences; he only finds a psychological explanation, based on known mental-emotional mechanisms, more convincing than the postulation of supernatural personalities. Following the scientific rule of economy of theory, which never postulates an additional unsupported theory when an accepted and supported one will satisfactorily explain an observed phenomenon, the scientific observer finds no need for supposing supernatural relationships.

Of course he recognizes the very strong desire for such relationships in most people in all known times and places, but regards that desire as irrelevant to reality.

It is probable that ever since he became able to think in abstract terms, man has always felt inferior and afraid. Actually man is by far superior to all other forms of life on this planet, and his usual cringing, piteous cries for help would surely appear ridiculous to any intelligence not conditioned by man's usual upbringing. The analogy with the child who refuses to be weaned from his mother's breast is inescapable. Man does not want to assume the responsibility of his own destiny, because he has been taught that he is helpless among the machinations of gods and devils and stars and all manner of supernatural forces which he cannot control. Of course there are many forces which he cannot, or cannot yet, control, but that does not make them supernatural. Of course, he cannot yet understand many natural phenomena, but that is not enough for them to be labeled ununderstandable and relegated to the field of faith.

Man has barely begun to explore the realities of this little planet and to reach out only a very little way into astronomical space. His knowledge of geology is still primitive, dealing with only a very little distance below the outer crust of the earth. His knowledge of the physiology and biology of the human is still far from complete, and that of human psychology and psychopathology has hardly begun.

In the face of all the evidence that he is only beginning to develop his ability to observe and understand even relatively simple things, man has dared the final presumption, and has claimed to know God.

Man is only beginning to learn how to think effectively, but throughout his development he has felt impelled to demand explanations for everything, no matter how far beyond any possibility of understanding with the knowledge currently available. Always someone would invent an explanation, which was then frozen into a faith and protected by taboo whenever it could be used to support some special interest.

For centuries man has been avoiding the responsibility for his own racial survival by laying it on his gods. He has prayed for rain and good crops while cutting down his forests, pasturing goats on his hills, denuding his land and, as rapidly as possible, manufacturing "dust bowls" and deserts.

He has prayed for health while ignoring the most elementary known measures for insuring it. Some of the most faithful to ancestral patterns still fight against the use of such proven aids to health as vaccines, toxoids, chlorination and fluoridation of drinking water, birth control and many others.

Man has long prayed for peace while insisting on retaining the very patterns of exclusive loyalties, narrow nationalism, and exploitation of others which make wars inevitable.

He subscribes publicly to doctrines of love and peace, while showing intolerance, hate and vengefulness in his usual behavior.

Worst of all, he has shown these inconsistencies to his developing children, teaching them specifically not to think through from cause to effect, not to accept responsibility for their own behavior, but to behave quite irresponsibly and depend on some magic or supernatural defense from the consequences of their own behavior.

It would seem that much, if not all, of man's self-produced worst problems comes from his having adventured far beyond his reach into the unknown, searching for answers that could only be invented.

If he could have taken, or could yet take, such answers as speculations, interim formulations, freely amenable to change with advancing knowledge, little if any harm would be done to his progress in knowledge.

It seems that man has always presumed to "know" many things which at the particular stage of his development he was, or is, not equipped to know. He has "known" the details of the lives of innumerable gods; that the sky was an inverted bowl over the flat earth; the details of man's appearance on the earth and even the date; the intentions of the creator God; the destiny of man; the conditions to be found in a life after death; what kinds of thinking, speech and behavior are pleasing to a watchful and always-listening God; and what kind will arouse his anger and vengeance.

It may well appear that man's "mortal sin" is that of presumption, a sin which has for thousands of years prevented his rational development to anything like his real potential.

As long as men will continue to teach their children unknowable things, or worse, things that are to be believed against all available objective evidence, so long will the children of men, when physically mature, avoid their uncomfortable responsibilities in favor of the most attractive fairy tale presented to them.

The people who have attained a stage of mental-emotional-social maturity appropriate to this generation have accepted the fact that they must learn to crawl before they can run, much less fly. They recognize the fact that there are innumerable unknowns, the answers to which are not available to man at this stage of his advance in knowledge.

It is recognizable now that almost no advances were made whenever or wherever faiths ruled medicine, astronomy, geology, social philosophy or any other aspect of human knowledge. Even religions were frozen and became increasingly rigid as long as faith was kept the paramount value. Every person who has tried to bring any religion more in line with man's current knowledge and aspirations has been called "heretic" by the faithful, including Jesus, who was indeed a heretic, and would be still if here now.

Fortunately, there are many and increasing numbers of heretics throughout the world now. Many are fighting lone battles, largely with their own early taught desire to conform, but many others have really freed themselves and are on the way to fearless living, with hope for ultimate world peace and social progress.

There are groups of such people in many countries. They may be identified as Humanists, Freethinkers, Rationalists, Unitarians or by many other names. What they have in common is the fact that they have not nailed any flag of faith to any fixed mast, but remain free to grow, to experiment with beliefs and to develop. They are concerned with taking the next appropriate steps in freeing man from his anchors in old absolutes, and with helping wherever possible in progress toward a rational, free and satisfying world. Very few of them have lost any of their reverence or awe in the face of the mysteries of the universe, and, I think, none of them has become socially irresponsible or selfish to an increased degree because of freedom from fear of punishment in the future, or from hope of reward for obedience.

There is one religious group, perhaps others, whose corporate and individual behavior does not show any signs of leaning on old faiths or revelations; neither do its members undertake missionary effort to convert others to their faiths nor accumulate power or wealth for a church. They have no priestly hierarchy, yet they are probably of all Christians the most Christlike. This group is known as the Society of Friends. Its members are commonly called Quakers, and they enjoy the trust, confidence and admiration of very large numbers of people outside their own community. It is often difficult, in discussing world affairs with a person not intimately known, to find any difference between the social attitudes of Quakers and of the members of the Humanist-Unitarian-Freethinker-Rationalist groups, though the pathway by which those attitudes are reached, and the beliefs supporting those attitudes, are very different. Perhaps the fact that they are all living in the present and the future, and not by the rules of the dead and irrelevant past, is the key to their present social constructiveness and very real social value. It is significant that the Quakers have no hierarchy, no creed and no church organization; all Quakers make their own interpretation of the Bible in the light of their common love for mankind.

XIV.

Education

THE EDUCATION of children has always been controlled largely by tradition. Whether the content and method of education was controlled by a central government, a local school board or board of education, or by a religious hierarchy, the effect usually has been to try to prepare children to live acceptably to a previous generation. Rarely indeed have children been given effective assistance in learning to live effectively in the future.

In a democracy, governmental control, in the hands of professional civil servants responsible to politicians, has had to accept restraint by the most numerous and vocal of the voters, always those who would follow their consciences in insisting on the same teaching for their children and other people's children that they themselves received. It is commonly accepted without examination that "what I was taught as a child" was good, and is still good. The local school board or board of education has generally shown the same attitudes.

Where a dictatorship or an absolute monarchy, or a hierarchy, is in control, of course the main purpose of education is to protect the power of the ruler or ruling groups and their vested interests.

These values demand suppression of freedom of thought and firm molding into a prescribed thinking and behavior pattern. It has often been necessary for distractions to be provided, particularly in institutions of higher education, to focus students' attention on quite irrelevant things while their minds were being warped and stunted by dogmatic and old certainties.

The process has produced some very strange examples of relative values. There are actually universities where it is not regarded as astonishing that a football coach can earn more than the president of the university! Indeed in some institutes of "learning," the coach is more admired and respected than the president, and the football "star" more than the best student. It should be noted that it is not the students who set these values, but the board of governors, senate, board of trustees or other governing body of the university, not, it is to be hoped, because of their own wishes, but in obedience to the wishes of the emotionally adolescent financial supporters of the university. Such values are often justified by the simple statement "The football team makes money."

It should be a matter of great concern to all of us that our values are so confused that our cultures pay television and movie actors and actresses more than we pay our schoolteachers, and we hardly notice the absurdity.

Is it any wonder that the children are not impressed with the value of education or of the development of the ability to think? Among many young people the possession of a pair of outsized breasts, or the ability to croon or sob off key, is inevitably regarded as a greater asset for living than academic qualifications, because their parents and the community are teaching them that dreadfully distorted scale of relative values.

The time is passing, but has not yet disappeared everywhere, when the janitor of the school was often paid more than the teachers. We have indeed gone to extremes to discredit the profession to whose long-suffering members we entrust our children's intellectual, emotional and social growth. It is an interesting commentary that in at least some of the Communist countries, university professors are said to be the most highly paid profession, followed by teachers of secondary and primary schools, and why not?

Is there any rational reason why a television or movie actress, or bond or stock trader, or lucky oil or uranium prospector, or automobile salesmen, or dance-orchestra leader, or song writer, or baseball player should be paid as much as a primary-school teacher? Which is more important to the sensible development of the human race and its hope of survival? Surely the vastly greater importance of the teacher can hardly be questioned by any reasonable person on any reasonable scale of values. It is not surprising that the values exemplified in "Western cultures" are regarded as mad in some other parts of the world.

The real tragedy is not that some relatively useless citizens are rewarded out of all proportion to their social value, nor even that many of our most valuable citizens are paid hardly enough to stay alive on; the disastrous effect is in the relative values children learn from their elders' attitudes. This is the education now being given to many millions of children.

It is not possible for our schoolteachers effectively to change the direction of that education; the teacher is himself discredited in the eyes of children by the system itself. Only parents and citizens generally can remove these heavy handicaps under which intelligent and conscientious teachers try to do their jobs, and there is little hope for a rational development of Western culture, or peace in the world, until enough citizens accept that responsibility.

Traditionally, and still in many schools, education has stressed the competitive, nonco-operative principle. Children have felt parental admiration and love when they "beat" the children of other parents, and it meant criticism and rejection, felt as loss of love, when they failed to do so. To compete successfully, to get ahead of others and stay ahead, as indicated by examination marks, has been regarded as of social value to parents. Many a teacher has been in trouble because low marks were awarded to the child of an important citizen or member of the school board. Nonco-operation has been taught by many teachers by not allowing children to help each other in school. The impression is commonly firmly made on children's minds that knowledge is an asset, not for use for common good, but to be hoarded for one's own competitive use. Why help a competitor, whom one must defeat in order to gain or keep the approval that all children really want and need from parents and teacher?

In reality assistance given by one child to another is of advantage to both. Often children learn more easily from the explanation of a contemporary and, more importantly, a helpful human relationship is established or developed. The child who assists another feels the pleasure of giving, tends to establish the habit, and becomes correspondingly less competitive and more co-operative, valuable for progress toward maturity.

Of course, education does not start at school. Much of the most significant establishment of values and attitudes has occurred before school age, and for this foundation of education the particular parents, the community and the culture are responsible. The construction of consciences has gone a long way before school age. In many people, whose personalities are of the more rigid type, there may be almost no growth of conscience after about six years of age. As very many people accept the judgment of their consciences without question throughout their lives, and as the basic conscience can only repeat back whatever was learned in childhood, and as conscience presumes to deal with all matters of right and wrong, it is clear that attitudes to which small children are exposed have tremendous importance for their future, and for the future of the community and the race.

It is not unimportant that a mother and father indicate by their obvious selection that the sports pages, the stock market quotations, the "comics," the astrological column, the social column, or the bloodiest murders or dirtiest scandals are the most significant of all the things happening in the world.

It is at this time that the firmest prejudices are implanted. The attitudes of parents may impose quite unreasonable convictions about any aspect of the whole human environment, or about the child's own body or mind or "soul."

One of the common distortions, usually at a very early age, has to do with sexual development. Variations in the ways this particular damage is done are many, but frequently the mother, always with the best of intentions and only passing on to the next generation what was done to hers, finds her child in bed or anywhere else engaged in a perfectly normal and healthy exploration of his total environment, as every intelligent child is likely to do. The trouble is caused by the fact that the object of the momentary interest of the child is the genito-urinary area of his or her own body, and the mother commonly has been given very dirty and mistaken attitudes about that part of all bodies. Her reaction may be one of obvious horror or disgust, with evidence of strong disapproval. Indeed she may overact her disapproval to impress the previously innocent child with the seriousness of the offense, and often, though unconsciously, the more effectively to demonstrate for herself her own purity.

A very common way of demonstrating such disapproval is to slap the child's hand, sometimes for the first time in a child's life, but this is regarded as a desperate situation and drastic action to save the child from unthinkable horrors is necessary. The words she uses to reinforce the already very impressive taboo are often "stop that, dirty, dirty, if you do that Mother won't love you any more."

Applied when very young, this is a dreadful threat to the basic source of security of the child and it is very effective. A taboo, guarded by fear of loss of love, is set up, which has the effect of rendering his body permanently dirty and disgusting, and of crippling one of his most important physiological and his most important biological functions. Many children are, by that one experience, made incapable of ever attaining a clean, healthy, enjoyable and stable marriage. Inevitably also, other important aspects of the development of the whole personality will be distorted and crippled by such a misleading experience.

It becomes necessary for the frightened child to stop his normal experiments whenever anyone else might see him, for fear of their hate, but the mother is often suspicious and usually, in the case of a healthy child, with good reason, that he is persisting secretly in his sinful ways. Therefore she watches him secretly to catch him doing it again. The next time she takes further steps to enforce the taboo by means of threats to tell the father, threats that such behavior will lead to insanity, or still worse, threats of the displeasure and vengeance of an all-powerful and all-seeing God, who watches the child all the time and can even see him in the dark and under the bedclothes.

If the unfortunate child believes that, he can only continue in his biologically prescribed but socially tabooed ways, and resign himself to damnation and torture in a future life and/or insanity in this one, or conform.

Often the child is told that he or she must put such things out of his, or her, mind in order to attain salvation and keep mother's love and his own sanity. This is very strong pressure on a helpless child to learn to "repress," not to think, to practice not thinking about painful things, and most unfortunately many children learn their lesson very well.

This ability not to think, to shut painful or difficult problems out of one's mind, destroys the proper functions of the imagination, and leaves one at the mercy of all sorts of appeals to emotion, without ability to explore truly the consequences of one's own projected behavior.

The social consequences of learning to repress while young are all destructive, but the mother feels that she has done her duty. Perhaps there should be more education in the facts of emotional-social development of children for prospective parents.

It would seem reasonable for parents to help their children's development by first themselves learning the true facts of emotional development of children and then determining to be honest with their children. How many mothers or fathers really believe that they themselves will be punished in a future life, or will go crazy, because they went through the same experiments when they were children, or for many years later? Is it not time that parents stopped lying to their children about this and other facts of life? It is known, and clearly, that genital play and masturbation are not harmful, except when they produce feelings of guilt and anxiety, which are always learned from someone else, usually parents. These are simply normal preparation for normal sexual function in maturity, as are play with dolls for motherhood, and membership in a "gang" for social integration later.

This is an exceedingly important aspect of child education, and it lies entirely in the area of responsibility of the parents. The schoolteacher, years later, cannot effectively correct parents' mistakes in this field, though the control of thinking, the inability to think through from cause to effect, and the ability to disregard consequences resulting from the parents' training may greatly complicate the child's life at school.

It is often in adolescence that such complications become more apparent, when they may show only as social tensions, or range through a great variety of symptoms up to "nervous breakdown," delinquency or even, though rarely, suicide.

The damage done by such parental attitudes is not confined to the sexual field alone, because the learned behavior of putting things that are offensive out of one's mind can prevent normal progress toward maturity in any aspect of life.

The children who have learned to repress, not to look at evidence but just to follow their consciences, often continue to be hero worshipers long past the childhood stage where that is normal, are easy, uncritical converts to the cure-all faiths of demagogues, look for salvation in new and authoritarian religions like communism, and are generally incapable of reaching the stage of development toward maturity appropriate for this generation.

It must be recognized that free, natural or uncivilized behavior is not the only alternative to repression of aggressive, sexual and other natural urges. Complete freedom to express natural urges in natural behavior will produce as many and as serious difficulties in the social and legal fields as will excessive repression in the emotional-mental field. Fortunately, this is not an either-or proposition. An effective compromise is quite possible in most cases.

The child needs to be able to accept all his urges as natural and normal and felt at the appropriate age by his parents also. He needs to learn early that in order to live peacefully with other people, he will have to conform to certain agreed forms of behavior, the local "customs of the natives," embodied in laws or conventions. Overt disregard of these local customs will make much trouble for him and for the people who love him. No one can successfully defy the agreed rules and at the same time count on the protection and support of the community, which everyone needs.

A child can be helped greatly if his parents indicate that there is nothing sacred or unchangeable about these local customs, and that many of them may not even be sensible, but also that they change only slowly and, in the meantime, have to be lived with.

It should be made very clear that society and the laws put no ban on feeling, wanting or thinking, only on behavior, which has to be controlled according to the legal code of the time and place. Incidentally, no law anywhere forbids masturbation except in public.

Such attitudes will go far to prevent the development of shame and guilt for being a human being with normal human urges, that "conviction of sin" which has warped so many personalities and is a major factor in the production of the well-known "inferiority complex."

Clear appreciation of the fact that the human is not born civilized, is not expected to have become so in early years by any code of law, and that only where his behavior relates to other people, animals or property need it conform to the local customs will ease many of the strains and difficulties every child and adult will meet on the road toward maturity. Above all, it should be clear to a child that his thinking and his imagination are his own private property, and he is free to use them freely to experiment in all imaginable directions.

These observations do not by any means exhaust possible consideration of all the common factors which tend to prevent development of children to the full potential of their basic equipment. For instance the pictures of the mutually supportive and noncompetitive roles of mothers and fathers in their biological, social, familial and personal fields of responsibility are very frequently much distorted. Competition between a mother and father for domination, or the successful assumption of domination by one or the other, can only hinder the sound development of a child, whether boy or girl. If a child is going to learn to live co-operatively, and learn it easily, he needs to learn the basic attitudes and techniques from his parents.

A child learns from his parents primarily by a process of identification with them. He grows into the patterns they provide, unless he comes into close contact with some other more understanding, trustworthy, approachable, loving and lovable person than his parents.

Because of this unconscious acceptance of the parents, particularly the parent of the same sex, as a model, many children become confused and their personalities develop strains and inconsistencies. This happens when there are inconsistencies between the attitudes of the two parents, or when one or the other shows inconsistencies between attitudes at one time and at another time, or between what he or she says and does. Innumerable examples are available of long and repeated arguments between parents, each defending his or her own pet way of spending money, or disciplining children, or arranging the furniture, or driving the car or almost anything else. Mature parents should recognize early that no one "wins" such arguments; one or the other may be talked down, or blackmailed by sulks, tears or silence, or temper, into grudgingly giving way, but that defeat will only demand a bigger victory at another time.

Parents should illustrate to their children sensible discussion of the factors involved and the reaching of a common decision, a pattern which is preached but not used by many parents. The only other kind of argument not harmful to the development of children is seen when parents who love each other discuss, even on an emotional basis, some such problem as what each would like to buy for the other out of limited funds, rather than something for himself or herself.

Of course, if parents agree that Mother should have a new fur coat, and Father new golf clubs or a hunting trip, but also that the family cannot afford a tricycle for little Jimmy, there is not much point in talking to Jimmy about his obligation to be generous to his little sister or playmates.

Similarly, it is useless for a father to try to inculcate social responsibility if he himself casually throws empty cigarette cartons or chocolate-bar wrappers out of his car window, or drops his cigarette or cigar butt into a urinal where someone else will have to pick it out. It is such casual behavior that demonstrates the parents' real attitudes and legitimizes selfish egocentric behavior on the part of the child, and the adult he will become. The father who behaves in such ways, or the child who learns attitudes from him, can hardly be expected ever to function successfully as a citizen of one world.

On the constructive side the responsibility of parents and teachers in development of children is far more extensive than most parents and some teachers admit.

Before a child ever reaches school, his education will have progressed a long way. He will already speak his native language correctly if his parents do and, if theirs is, his vocabulary will be adequate to his environment and stage of development. If his parents have done their job well up to that point, the child will be well oriented in many important areas and a good foundation laid for assistance in further development of knowledge and attitudes by the teacher. If the parents have not fulfilled these responsibilities, the child and the teacher will be handicapped seriously.

There are many fields of human knowledge in which the child should be at home before school age, not completely informed, of course, but aware of progress in knowledge and to some degree interested.

One of these fields of relationship through which it is necessary to develop on the way from infancy toward maturity is that of time. Ignorance and mistaken certainties have combined to confuse the time relationship of most of the world's people.

When a baby is born he has no conception of time. Conscious existence is made up only of his feeling at the moment and he must develop a long way to reach a mature relationship with time, appropriate to this stage of human development. Gradually he becomes aware of time and learns to look backward and forward in time: he remembers satisfactions of yesterday and begins to hope for, and later to plan for, satisfaction tomorrow. Yesterdays and tomorrows gradually stretch out into weeks, months and years, and will continue to expand with some help, and unless discouraged or stopped by parental ignorance or prejudice.

No child's experience of the past should stop at some mythological date which has no support except old tribal folk tales, with "Adam" and "Eve," for example. In many Christian churches and Sunday schools nowadays the time issue is avoided, but in many annotated Bibles the date of creation is still baldly stated as 4004 B.C. Of course it would be very difficult to support the faith in the literal infallibility of the Bible if it were to be examined in the light of the facts established by geologists, astronomers and anthropologists in recent generations, but those facts have not yet gained acceptance in many Sunday schools and churches.

Children are entitled to be introduced by their parents to the simpler wonders of geology and fossils and astronomy and to some idea of the time scale that goes with them, including man's short existence of half a million years or so in comparison with that of many other animals which flourished for many millions of years before that.

Only with a background of the awareness of the enormous extent of time, and of biological development, even on this very young earth, is it possible for man to see himself, and his stage of development of knowledge, in anything like true perspective, but to gain that awareness he needs to start in early childhood.

The normally developing child also adventures into the future. While still quite young he should be able to overcome some of the immediacy of the demands of his infancy and to forgo minor satisfactions today for better ones tomorrow. Gradually, if his parents are forward looking and will help him, he will develop the ability to plan his future course in terms of his total satisfactions on a lifetime basis. Of course if his parents buy things they cannot afford on a time-payment basis, sometimes losing possession or finding they wear out before something is paid for, or if they spend such a proportion of their income for immediate satisfactions that other, more important things cannot be obtained, or if they live in ways that indicate that they consider today's pleasure more important than greater pleasures that might be obtained sometime in the future, the child's development in this field will be handicapped.

Given appropriate help by parents before and during school years, the teacher should be able to continue the job so that by the later teen years or thereabouts it should be normal to be able to function reliably in imagination about ten years ahead of the moment's stage of growth. Education for the complexities of any adult responsibilities will need at least ten years of preparation. By the age of sixteen or seventeen or so, any intelligent young man or woman should be able to know what kind of person he or she intends to be, what sort of relationship he or she proposes to establish with the community, and with what and how big a community. It should be possible then to choose the type of training that will lead toward the projected goal and to persevere in obtaining that training.

Much of the most important work being done in the world requires people who can function in terms of future generations, doing constructive work which they realize will not benefit, or often even please, the present generation, but is calculated to begin or encourage progress which will bear fruit far in the future. The world, and every culture, need far greater numbers of such people than are available.

It is the people who have not developed fully in the time relationship that demand immediate solutions to all questions. They are the people who want to discard the United Nations because it has "failed." Could any reasonable mature person expect any arrangement between self-centered, nationalistic, impatient governments to do more than the United Nations has done in a few short years? Only those who do not think and feel in terms of time and growth, who want all solutions to spring ready-made from an organizational womb, without a long growing period of parturition, the inevitable labor pains and a period of helpless infancy and adjustment of the offspring.

Of course it is natural and inevitable that hungry people of the world should be impatient and demanding of immediate results from international organization, but the fact is that most of the people of the underdeveloped hungry countries are not too displeased with the progress being made by the United Nations and its specialized agencies. It is largely the well-fed, prosperous people who seem to have expected an immediate solution from the United Nations for all their anxieties and infantile demands for something now that still must be evolved by experiment, sacrifice, heavy payment and painful growth. The orientation in time of such people is grossly deficient. The coming generation will need a much better time relationship if there is to be hope of their solving enough of the problems produced by the ignorance and neglect of their ancestors, even of their parents.

In the light of past and future eternity, or as much of it as man is capable of appreciating up to now, one's own little local and temporary troubles tend to become of less emotional concern, and the welfare of the race to be seen in better perspective.

Just as in relation to time, there is far to go on the way from infancy toward security in relation to space. Again the infant has no conscious spatial relationship. There is no distinction between here and there, no concept of difference. To feel at home in the immensity of even the relatively tiny part of universal space which is appreciable by man at this stage of his knowledge requires a long development. That development also needs to start in early childhood. It is important that no concepts limiting space should be imposed on any young child, and also that the unknown areas of space should not be peopled with imaginary persons who can affect human lives.

For many millions of children space away from the earth holds infinite varieties of possible or inevitable interference with human destiny. Some have learned that somewhere aloft is a heaven peopled with God and Jesus and saints and angels and all the people who have died who were good, or were bad and repented. For many children all their actions are watched by ghostly observers, and for some their badnesses are all written down in a big book for reference at a judgment day after they die. Complicating all this for some children are the personality and influences ascribed to some stars by astrology, in the absurdities of which parents show their children their belief.

Somewhere downward, in or below the earth, is for many children another peopled world, for some of them very clear cut and precise. There Satan rules and spends eternity with all his attendant devils in torturing bad people. The relationship between God up above and Satan down below, while never precisely stated, seems to be one of co-operative partnership on a more or less even basis. Certainly, someone has to torture the bad people, or what is the advantage of being good? There is always the possibility of last-minute reprieve by an Act of Grace and forgiveness on the part of God, but that is unpredictable and not to be counted on.

Of course any intelligent child who has been taught to believe any of these fantastic old myths will be afraid of the dark and of many other harmless things. After he has succeeded in repressing the actual basis of his fear by putting all these threatening things out of his conscious mind, there will not necessarily be left any conscious belief in their existence, but all unknown areas will tend to be peopled by vague but anxiety-producing concepts.

Very few children learn in any understandable terms that the universe is neutral, neither appreciably friendly nor unfriendly toward man, nor toward anything else, but this should be learned early if a child is going to learn to live in the reality of his total environment. No star, or god, or saint, or devil will protect him from the consequences of his own behavior or vindictively punish him for transgressing the local and temporary agreed rules of behavior, though other humans may try to do so.

Shortly after birth the child begins to explore space with hands, eyes, ears, skin, nose and mouth. For much of his early exploration he needs no help except freedom to explore, and particularly to explore all of his own body.

Every normal child's natural drive is to explore in all directions, everywhere he can reach or see. He will extend these explorations as far as he is allowed to do, and at early stages needs a certain amount of unobtrusive protection wherever there are real risks, such as ill-tempered dogs, poisonous snakes, strong electric currents, pots of boiling soup or water, etc. A child should not be protected from hurting himself by falling off things he has climbed onto, unless he is very low in intelligence. If he is allowed to climb and fall, soon enough he will not fall far and will not be hurt. Even a fall downstairs will almost never hurt a small child at all seriously unless the experience has been postponed for too long by overprotection. Even at the expense of a little passing pain every child needs to learn that his own behavior produces inevitable consequences. He can never become a responsible citizen until he does learn that, and he needs to start that learning early.

Physically the exploration of a small child can now be, and usually now is, much more extensive than in past generations, but correspondingly less intensive. The modern child commonly covers more ground than his ancestors did, and gets a far greater variety of impressions, from car windows, through television, even from planes, and is exposed to much greater numbers of ununderstandable things, many of which he is usually not allowed to touch.

Probably there is no extensive area for the modern child in which he is very familiar with all the objects to be seen and felt as there was for his great-great-grandfather in a pioneer cabin, or confined to the area which could be covered on foot or by horses. In past generations things moved comparatively slowly and there was time to see and to think about them. Clearly the development of children now will be different from that of our ancestors, but much study still must be undertaken before all the elements of child development are understood.

It would seem probable that in an environment in which so many things move and change so rapidly the child of this generation will need more close dependable parental contact, particularly with the mother, in order to help him keep his feelings of security and belonging. Given that feeling of security in his own immediate environment which can come only from dependable love, other places will be a challenge to exploration and not fearful or threatening, unless some of the hobgoblins mentioned previously are introduced into the unknown areas. In that case fear is inevitable in an intelligent child.

Before school age, parents should have helped their children to explore superficially all the space of this earth; the details can be filled in by the schoolteachers later. A globe in the home is a great help for this phase of basic education. By five years of age a child can well profit by some discussion of various common theories of what lies under the surface of the earth. The ancient myth of hell might well be kept for study at university level, where it belongs in cultural anthropology and theology.

Astronomical space, outside this one planet, is a difficult concept for most adults, but it may be found much easier if introduced in childhood. This is a part of everyone's environment which is seen every day and night; to ignore it or to people it with magic is unfair to children, whose development is going to be difficult enough without misleading complications.

If this aspect of a child's development is assisted successfully by parents and teachers, he will feel himself living in a world, in a universe, not just in a house, or a town, or even a country. He will be much less likely to be an ardent partisan of any one place in adulthood and will be helped greatly toward attainment of the ability to become a world citizen.

Among the very important areas of development from infancy toward maturity is that of relationship with other people. At birth the infant has no conscious relationships, not even with himself. It seems that he is not conscious of any distinction between his mother and himself. The feel of the mother, her skin, her hands or breast, is a part of himself and apparently his identification with her is very close. Gradually he appreciates the fact of his own separate existence, though there may be a long persisting reluctance to give up

the security inherent in that oneness with his mother. The acceptance of separateness needs to develop slowly; too early or too sudden weaning, refusal to hold the child frequently enough and for
long enough in close physical contact, too early attempts at toilet
training or any other attempts to force the pace can complicate the
whole process and may even do serious permanent harm to the child.
On the other hand, undue prolongation of the nursing months into
years can also produce developmental complications.

Having established his own separateness, discovered himself, the
child's chief or only external value for some time is his relationship
with his mother, and the conditions of that relationship are important for the whole process of development, emotional, physical, mental and social. Many studies of recent years show that interruptions
of the child-mother relationship at an early age will slow or halt
various aspects of the child's development, and under certain circumstances may produce deep regression and even irreparable damage.

In some parts of the world mothers invariably take their very ill
children to the hospital themselves, and stay with them throughout
the time they are there, doing almost all the necessary nursing under
the instructions of the trained hospital nurses. Wherever that is done
there is good evidence that the child recovers from any illness more
quickly and without interruption of his emotional development.
Many of the so-called underdeveloped countries are far ahead of
the so-called highly developed countries in this, as in some other of
their cultural patterns.

In some of these same "underdeveloped" countries some maternity
wards are far better equipped than is at all usual in the "highly
developed" countries to facilitate the highly desirable close relationship between baby and mother. In such wards upward extensions of
the posts at the foot of the mother's bed support a swinging cradle,
so that the baby is never out of the mother's reach. At the first movement or sound from the baby, the mother can raise her foot and
rock the cradle with almost no effort. It is very easy for her to reach
down and take the baby into her arms, restoring it to the cradle
only after it is asleep. The mother's and the baby's charts hang on
the side of the cradle facing the aisle between the beds. These

and the baby are in a very convenient position for any nursing care, which is minimal, that the mother cannot provide herself. The saving in nurses' time, hospital space, traffic and expense is very great, but these considerations are far less important than are the great emotional advantages enjoyed by babies in such wards over those separated from their mothers for long periods in sterile but lonesome nurseries, as is still usually the case in European and North American hospitals.

The primary need of every baby, following only the absolute requirements of sufficient food, warmth and shelter to maintain life and growth, is dependable, constant, uncritical love from the mother or a substitute mother.

If he does not feel that love, or if he feels that love is contingent on his behavior, he will feel unloved, unwanted, rejected and his development will suffer. Such feelings give the baby the impression that the world is a cold, hard, unfriendly, cruel place, and induce a tendency in the child to retreat from life or on the other hand to fight for his status. Either of these reactions is unfortunate and will make much trouble for the child, and often for his family, later in life. He may be inclined to be seclusive, shut in, easily hurt, unable to make friends or, on the other hand, to join some militant group to fight against almost anything, but rarely constructively for anything, or his difficulty may take the form of social defiance, delinquency or criminality. His whole development in this important area of relationship with other people will have been hampered if he does not find sufficient of the right kind of expressions of love in babyhood.

If this love is found, and can be counted on to be constant, the child tends to establish certain attitudes. They might be expressed as: "The world is a friendly place; people are kind and dependable; I am acceptable and loved; there are pleasant experiences and adventures ahead and throughout life; I do not have to be afraid of anything." Such a child expects friendship and finds it everywhere, because he has no need to hold back and make other people come all the way to him, but can go all the way in confidence to meet other people in friendliness. He will tend to make friends easily, his feelings will not be hurt easily, and when he does occasionally meet a person incapable of real friendliness he will recognize that person as an unfortunate exception and sympathize with him in his disability, or at least he will do all these things far more easily than can the unloved child.

It is at this stage that the child who is pressed too early into conformity with the local customs, so that his behavior will bring credit to his parents, risks the establishment of the well-known "inferiority complex" which can be such a curse to him later and throughout his life. It develops in some such way as this: the child is behaving in some perfectly normal way, sucking his thumb or exploring his genito-urinary area, or has not waited for what his mother happens to regard as the proper time or place for evacuation of bladder or bowel, or is reaching for something breakable, and the mother shows her disapproval in a tone of voice, and facial expression, or even physically by a slap. This first new threatening tone of voice, expression, or actual assault is a shock to any child and it withdraws physically and emotionally. The infant's feeling is that the mother has turned against him, has become a threat, an enemy. The accompanying words, "bad, bad boy," will not be understood at first and attain meaning only when he compares them with the "good boy" which he wins when he has conformed to the particular customs to which his mother happens to subscribe. Of course the child has no way of knowing that some of these customs are arbitrary and local, and maybe matters only of his mother's convenience, or of her dirty feelings about genitals and sex. A small child can only accept these accidental variants as absolutes.

He knows that when he is doing what he wants to, when he wants to, is the time he is called bad and is hit, and not loved by his mother. It is when he is conforming to the arbitrary code of which he so far knows very little except that it is not natural to him that he is called good, and is loved and feels secure when he behaves in that way. These facts produce in many children a fear and reluctance to explore, a tendency to withdraw into themselves, to avoid new experience because they don't know what the rules for new situations are, and they may be called bad and be threatened with loss of love or assault. The safe behavior is behavior restricted to patterns previously proved acceptable, so no risks are run and there is no need to feel afraid.

But whether the child likes it or not he is going to be forced into many new situations. Such a child tends to be reluctant and fearful of going to school and may suffer acutely when he has to do so. He may hold onto his mother in real panic when faced by new situations. It is never the real situation of which he is afraid, but fear of loss of love of his mother, or by this time of his father, also. All unknowns have already been made fearful; he is by this time usually afraid of the dark, though he commonly does his best to conceal it from everyone.

His tragedy is that he has come to believe that he himself is naturally "bad," and so he is fearful of any new circumstances which might show up that badness, that is, under which he might behave naturally, instead of in whatever unknown ways the local customs might find acceptable and would call "good." He believes that anyone who comes to know what he is really like will despise and hate him.

The concept of sin which he may meet at home or in Sunday school about this time reinforces this fear very strongly, and also pushes him strongly into conformity. The still more damaging concept of the all-seeing and all-knowing God and the "fear of God," which he learns is standard for all good people, leaves him no alternative to trying to keep even his thinking good. If he succeeds he will use that same method of repression to avoid painful or even only difficult thinking as long as he lives. It is not to be expected that he will be able to think clearly about threatening world conditions later. He will want to leave all such uncomfortable responsibilities to a "leader," a political "hero," or a "God," while he acquires virtue, or the feeling of virtue, by conforming to the regimenting demands of the "good" people and whatever authority they may support. Of course at any stage he may rebel against all these controls, still not thinking matters out for himself, but commonly being led into rebellion by a gang leader, or demagogue, who will preach and offer another competing authority in the name of freedom, or of hate of authority.

Of course most of these reactions are not distinct and clear cut. They may often alternate; conformity, with an emotional orgy of self-criticism, penitence and expiation, may take turns with delinquency, drunkenness or any conceivable type of antisocial behavior. Refuge of a sort is sometimes found in illness and dependence on others, or in chronic complaint and accusation against wife, or husband, or children of withholding love.

Any of these, and of innumerable other surface manifestations of a buried inferiority complex, with its multitudinous psychopathological complications, can stem from the "conviction of sin" in small childhood. All of such personality distortions prevent the establishment of mature relationships with other persons, either male or female.

Perhaps the most important obligation of parents to their children is in this area of interhuman relationships, an area in which most parents have had no training, even no appreciation of their deficiencies.

True relationship with reality is another necessity for any adult, in order that he may be able to carry his responsibilities adequately, as a person, as a parent or as a citizen of his own country and of the world. The philosophical question, "What is reality?" is not relevant to this discussion, if it is relevant to anything at this stage of human development. It is only the philosopher who does not know what reality is, and this is not a discussion for philosophers. Of course the knowledge of reality is extended with every piece of honest reporting of honest observation and experiment. It is not extended by revelation or intuition, except as the knowledge of the intuitive process is extended. Intuition is a reality, it exists, but its results may be quite at variance with reality. It may be no more than wishful thinking.

It would seem that the most useful role of parents in this area of child development is to ensure the freedom of the child to use his own power of observation intelligently, and to keep it from being distorted by the local cultural coloration, prejudices and taboos. The parental responsibility may be put briefly as "Don't lie to children about anything." Most people will agree that that is a sound injunction, but many parents who would agree nevertheless lie to their children extensively, only they don't call it lying. There seems to be a common attitude that anything taught by their own parents to them is not a lie, when they teach their children the same thing, no matter how incompatible with facts that teaching may be. Many parents have two quite different standards of honesty, one for children and one for themselves. They can, and do, actually punish their children for far less serious lying than they themselves indulge in freely, and without noticing any inconsistency in themselves, or feeling at all guilty.

It should be recognized that lies to children of low intelligence are relatively unimportant, because they do not think through them to any of their implications, but leave the lies more or less isolated without any extensive distortion of associated attitudes.

A few examples of common parental lies and some discussion of the effects on some intelligent children may be useful. One type of lie often believed to be harmless, indeed often defended on the score of protection or stimulation of the child's imagination, I have often illustrated by the following true incident.

Two boys, about six and four years of age or a little less, were overheard, without their knowledge, while playing together. The older boy was repeating, "Don't be silly, it does not," while the younger, obviously in trouble, not quite crying but with lips trembling, repeated, "It does so, it does so," and then, putting his hands over his ears, said, "I won't listen to you." The bigger boy pulled the smaller's hands away from his ears and shouted, "It does not. How can the sun go to bed? There isn't any bed in the sky, is there?" The smaller boy now in tears and clearly desperately unhappy, whimpered, "The sun does so go to bed at night. My daddy told me so." Of course his unhappiness and obvious fear were the consequences of his first dawning awareness that his daddy had lied to him and that he could not be depended upon any more.

If the well-meaning father had explained only that the sun was "gone" when it set at night, no trouble would have been caused and no risk of loss of his son's confidence and trust. The boy, a very intelligent child, would not have had to set up a picture, taking for granted its reality, of the sun climbing or being boosted into bed, being kissed good night and so on. I have heard of at least one even more enthusiastic liar among fathers who, when questioned, told his trusting son that the moon tucked the sun into bed before it came up.

Another example of parental distortion of reality is the common perversion of the old Santa Claus myth. Many parents still teach that excellent old myth as though it were true. Myths taught as symbolic of human development or human qualities can be useful, but taught as true can only be destructive. Many parents who, theoretically, are against lying to children still mislead their children with unblushing lies, converting what should be delightful and imaginative play to a real menace to the intellectual and emotional integrity of the child and to his development.

During these crucial developmental years, when it is most important that the child should be learning to differentiate clearly between fantasy and reality, to have parents who consistently and in a highly organized way combine to misinform and fool him can hardly be helpful. He needs to be learning about cause and effect, about how things really work in the world he is so busily exploring, how to observe truly and to reason effectively on the basis of those observations, how to foresee consequences and to behave in ways that will produce desired results, to exercise his reasoning powers and develop confidence in his own independent use of those powers. All this is vital equipment for the mature person, and there is so far for the child to travel, so much to do, that parents, indeed all adults, should try to help children, not to hinder them in the big job they have to do.

If a child at three or four or sometimes even five years of age is to believe, on the basis of his trust in his parents, the only source of security for him, that a great fat man can come down a chimney which he can see for himself is only a few inches in size; if that man can bring with him a great pack of toys, perhaps even a bicycle, or toboggan, or a big doll's house, or in some families a Christmas tree, and without any soot coming down with him; if he can call at all the houses in the world, or at least everywhere there are good children, in one night; if he can fly through the air complete with reindeer and sleigh; if he can know each child in the world and keep a record of the balance between the goodness and the badness of every child, then there is no possible differentiation between fantasy and reality.

Anything resting on parental trustworthiness has to be believed at the risk of loss of love and consequent deep anxiety, so the child has no choice but to swallow all these lies. From the point of view of his memory they become original premises. He has always believed and never questioned them in early years, and has been building his picture of how things work, what the world is like, on that misinformation. By the time his own observation, if free, would inform him that these things are not and cannot be true, he has already had to refuse to see, and to think, to avoid the painful and dangerous consequences inherent in his recognition of the untrustworthiness of his parents. A small child simply dare not accuse his mother and father, even in his own mind, of lying to him consistently for years; the implications are too fearful. "If you can't trust daddy and mommy, you can't ever trust anybody in the world." The alternative that some children try to hold to for a while is the belief that the parents themselves are fooled, but that soon leads to conclusions just as hard to take, that they are fools and incapable of seeing facts.

Consequently very many children force themselves to go on believing in the reality of the myth until irreparable damage is done, and until they have to choose between belief in parents or in other, usually older, children. Even then, after they have discarded their parents as unreliable or fools, and have accepted their contemporaries as more trustworthy, most children pretend to their parents that they still believe the parental lies. They have learned that to believe is good; whether the subject of the belief is the truth or a lie is irrelevant. This has been the teaching of their parents.

Very few children ever ask their parents why they engaged in all this lying. That would be like an accusation, and children are afraid to embarrass their parents, particularly if it appears to them that discovery of parental perfidy would be followed by punishment or withdrawal of love and protection. As one child put it, "They cannot want you to know the truth or they wouldn't lie to you."

Santa Claus, with all the attendant delights of giving and receiving, of surprise and decorations and festivity and love and security within the family, can be enriching and satisfying, as long as no magic or distortion of thinking is involved. Children greatly enjoy "pretends" and have no fear of anything pretended as long as they don't have to believe the unbelievable. Played as a game, everyone pretending together, and clearly knowing that they are all pretending, there is fun for everyone, no frightening implications or loss of trust in parents, and no necessity to repress the truth and teach one-self perversion of intellectual processes.

Another example of distortion of reality, very commonly seen, is reported in a news item dated November 10, 1955: "Mrs. J. F. has given up talking over Sunday school lessons with her daughter. The little girl came home and said, 'The teacher told us that before children are born they are dust and that they return to dust when they die. Is that true, Mommy?'

"Mrs. F. replied that if it was taught at Sunday school it was true. 'Why do you ask, honey?'

" 'Well,' the youngster drawled, 'I just looked under my bed and someone is either coming or going.' "

Most people will see the joke in the third paragraph of this little story, but miss the tragedy in the first two. "Mrs. F. has given up talking over Sunday school lessons with her daughter." A taboo has been set up. The child will recognize an area in which reason is discounted, and which must be avoided to save mother embarrassment. She can no longer trust her mother, and will go to other people for explanations.

Mrs. F., when asked in all honesty and confidence by her daughter if this absurd statement is true, assures the trusting child that "if it was taught at Sunday school it was true." Of course it is not true; it is a lie. People are not dust before they are born. They are ova and sperms and genes and multiplying cells, and bear no slightest resemblance to dust. The child is being grossly misinformed at Sunday school, and her mother, who should protect her from lies, is prepared to back up those lies, "sight unseen." Whatever the Sunday school teacher says, she will support, apparently just because it is taught in Sunday school and is therefore "good," not true, but "good."

A little girl or boy has very little chance of protecting the integrity of his own thinking against such a combination of authority. The child and her hope of attaining maturity are sacrificed to the faith that did the same thing to the mother and to the Sunday school teacher, the faith that if it was taught in Sunday school it was true.

In the ordinary everyday experience of most children we can see innumerable examples of these intellect-distorting lies. Reading columns on astrology in front of children; subscribing to ridiculous superstitions such as black cats, number 13, touching wood to placate some jealous and watchful god or spirit or demon when one boasts of, or even mentions, success or good luck; throwing spilled salt over one's shoulder; being careful to see a new moon first over one or the other shoulder; supporting the old tribal myth that there was one first man named Adam, with a wife made out of a rib—all these and many, many others of their kind teach a child that there is super-natural interference, from somewhere outside human perception or control, with everything. Cause and effect and reality have no mean-ing, and any attempt to maintain intellectual integrity is dangerous, and even evil.

While most of this trouble seems to come from the parents' neces-sity to conform, not to step out of line, part of it apparently comes from their great reluctance to admit to children that there is anything they do not know, and from their conviction that children need a firm, certain answer to all questions for their greater security. It is indeed an impoverished personality that cannot afford to admit igno-rance, and children, given security in the love of trustworthy, honest parents, do not need any other certainties. They can well afford to be given a true explanation of the real situation, involving a variety of explanations advanced by different people, or religions or cultures or ideologies.

For instance, it is quite misleading to give a child the impression that religion means just one sect, or one religion. There are very many religions, each with its revelation, its dogmas and its rituals, or its escape from all these to humanism or rationalism. The sect or religion to which the parent is attached commonly is accidental, in that he or she was born into it. Sometimes the parent has left some other group for the present affiliation, to find some particular sup-port or emotional necessity which he or she happens to need. That is no indication that the same dogmas or ritual will be what the child needs when he grows up.

Would it not be fairer to the child to show him something of all the major religions and of their principal variations, leaving him free to adopt whichever he finds most acceptable, if any, when he has developed the emotional-intellectual capacity to make a free and wise choice for himself? Some people will object that then the child will not be religious at all, but that is to say that acceptance of a religion is likely for only underdeveloped minds. If refuge is taken in the myth of saving the child's soul from perdition, of course there is no argument possible, because that takes the discussion out of the rational field into that mystic zone where anything can happen or be believed.

It is very clear, however, that what the world needs is thinkers, not believers, and the child brought up to know the essential elements of all religions will be much more likely to be able to think independently, constructively and for the welfare of all kinds of people.

A very real and pressing necessity for the very survival of the human race is large numbers of people who can, and will, face facts, no matter how uncomfortable or threatening, and will take the responsibility of thinking and acting independently of past attitudes and appropriately to the world as it is now. A generation brought up to believe in a god of the universe, who nevertheless enjoys being praised and "glorified" by mankind, which has existed for only a moment of time on one tiny satellite of one solar system among billions of others, can hardly be expected to be able to force themselves to think truly about the complexity of racial survival. It is so much easier to conform to earlier learned patterns and to leave all responsibilities to the "leaders" and to God.

There is no evidence that a trust in God, or that faithful prayer, has prolonged the lives of religious members of armed forces as compared with the atheists or agnostics, nor that there has been any supernatural interference with the effects of atomic bombs. Wholesale death at Hiroshima did not discriminate between the prayerful Buddhists and Christians and the atheists.

Belief in an all-knowing, all-loving and all-powerful personal god can be very comforting to the frightened, but at the sacrifice of emotional-intellectual-social integrity and social value in the highest sense.

The concept of a personalized god, in direct personal relationship with a single person, aggrandizes that person out of all reasonable proportion, and fortifies the basic statement in the Presbyterian catechism, "Man's chief end is to glorify God and enjoy him forever." Any god of the universe who could support such an entirely selfish, egotistic reason for the existence of the human race is not worthy of respect, or believable to a free mind.

Mature interpersonal relationship on a world basis is not possible for any person who can believe anything so incompatible with human responsibility for the destiny of the race.

Relationship with things, another area in which long, slow growth toward maturity is necessary, is largely dependent on growth in relation to reality, and may be mixed with relationship to persons. Here, too, children can be misled by parents and others to the detriment of their development and of their later social value.

An example may be useful. A man in his thirties, intelligent, physically fit but unable to hold any of a long succession of jobs, was referred for treatment by a personnel supervisor. From some jobs he had been discharged and from others he had quit. He felt that he had been discriminated against, treated badly, "framed," or blamed unfairly, in every job he had ever held. He blamed several foremen for "being against" him, but could never find any reason why they should have been. It appeared that it was not only employers or bosses with whom he had trouble but sooner or later with everyone with whom he had come in contact, including landladies of boarding houses, fellow boarders and members of his own family. He had been a member of a union but quit it because of the unfriendliness and antagonism of other members.

There was nothing remarkable in the history of his emotional development except a rather unusually selfish father and a mother and other close relatives who had done everything possible in his childhood to protect him from the consequences of, and responsibility for, his own behavior.

The father was an example of a common type of semicivilized man, who puts his own whim of the moment above anyone else's convenience or feelings. He threw his empty cigarette packages down on the street, or on people's lawns, or out of car windows, into urinals or anywhere else he happened to be when he finished the package. He parked his car in places that would block other cars; he would stand in the middle of a sidewalk to talk with someone else and force other people to go around them; he would bully defenseless waiters in restaurants. Altogether he presented to his son a picture of complete disregard of other people's feelings and even rights. He was able to afford such behavior because he was a "successful" builder and contractor who was ruthless and tough but always within the law.

The mother had always protected her small son from falling off anything or from adventuring beyond her own protection, and when he was hurt, as all active children are hurt, she taught him that it was not his fault by blaming whatever had hurt him. He remembered an incident which was repeated with variations many times and throughout the early years of his life. At an early age he was running through the living room and fell over a low stool or seat. Naturally he cried, and was quite soundly taken into his mother's arms to be comforted, but then his mother said that she would "spank the bad stool for tripping her darling boy." Then she seriously slapped the stool and encouraged her son to do the same. He remembered on at least one occasion, and with his mother's approval, hitting something with a stick, perhaps a box in the cellar or garage, for scratching his leg. His aunts and grandmother also taught this same method of avoiding responsibility by blaming it on inanimate things.

He felt that some things were malevolent, would hurt him if they could, got in his way on purpose, and that they should be punished. His own behavior was always perfectly innocent; he was just doing whatever he wanted to do and had been doing just that all his life, but all sorts of things got in his way, people also; he "never got the breaks"; he was always being "picked on." He cursed his car for having something wrong with it when it was just suffering from his own neglect.

He had never thought of his own behavior as responsible for all his misfortunes; he was still just innocently doing anything he wanted to do, as his mother had so convincingly taught him was right from infancy. This is another way of lying to children about reality, personifying inanimate things and endowing them with human character and intentions. The inevitable handicapping of the child and later adult is obvious.

Another distortion of relationship with things comes from the injunction, repeated millions of times to children, "Don't touch," or "Mustn't touch." The impression made on intelligent children is that there is some unknown danger in "touching." Actually there are very few things that a child should not be allowed to touch. There is real reason for not touching a hot stove, or pot, or electric toaster, or heater, or any electric appliance or even switch when in a bathtub or while also touching a tap or radiator or anything else that is grounded, but a child should be allowed to touch and feel anything that will not hurt him seriously. For instance, it is helpful to the child if a parent touches an electric-light bulb which is hot, withdraws his hand quickly and says, "Hot." After that the child should be allowed to touch it if he wants to; any hurt will be very slight, and he will have had the advantage and satisfaction of firsthand experience. Certainly he should not be urged or at all encouraged to do anything that will hurt him, but he should not be stopped from experimenting harmlessly.

To help a child to learn how to deal with breakable things is worth some effort. If the mother or father will take the trouble to pick up a glass, obviously very carefully (an inexpensive one is best for training purposes), saying at the same time, "Careful, careful," and then encouraging the child also to carry the same glass carefully, the lesson will be much more constructive than the common "Don't touch" method. "Careful" shows confidence in the child's ability to handle the glass, whereas "Don't touch" conveys the threat of some unknown danger and of parental disapproval, and private experimental touching may be undertaken under great tension or defiantly. Under such pressures, because the action will be hasty and anxious, if the thing touched is delicate it is likely to be broken, the child punished for being disobedient, and the taboo further strengthened. If the thing touched is not damaged, the child learns that parental warnings can be disregarded safely, and a further step in the "debunking" of the parent has been taken. Of course parents who so mislead their children should be "debunked," but the process also weakens any positive values they might have had for the child. A child's classifications tend to be general and ruthless. If a parent is caught lying once, he or she is never really quite believed again. This also is probably a good thing in the case of parents who are chronic liars.

In some very intelligent children who are forbidden to touch, a real anxiety can be seen about the dangers of touching. If this happens to be reinforced by a taboo on "touching himself," meaning exploring his genital area, the effects can be greatly exaggerated. Incidentally this use of the word "self" to mean genital area, as in "touching yourself," "playing with yourself," "self-abuse" and so on can reinforce self-hate, self-distrust and feelings of inferiority to an important degree. I remember a boy who had heard a man admired as "selfless," and thought it meant that the man had no genital organ.

Children need to be helped to learn to touch and to handle even breakable things without fear, and with confidence. "Don't touch" should be reserved for really dangerous things, with which experimentation is too risky, and touching really would be harmful.

Relationship with authority is a further area in which long growth must take place and in which many children are led astray.

In some cultures obedience has been set up as a first moral principle. In Hitler's Germany it was possible for the government to set up and operate extermination camps, experiments in poisoning prisoners and killing them serially to learn more of the effects of poisons, and torture clinics to force confessions from underground workers because the German children for generations had been taught absolute and unquestioned obedience from small childhood.

There are circumstances in which unhesitating and unquestioned obedience are highly desirable, but they are rare. In a ship on fire at sea, in a boat in a storm, particularly a sailing boat, in catastrophic situations such as may be produced by floods, earthquakes, tornados, artillery or bombing bombardments, or atomic bomb explosions, and in military organizations, prompt unquestioning obedience to the authority in charge is almost invariably desirable. In such circumstances there is not time to consider opinions, points of view and varying experience to obtain better decisions and co-ordination. The decisions must be made and co-ordination ensured by one person or a co-ordinated organization in charge. It is important that every mature person should be able to submit himself to authority when necessary. It is also important that he should be able to obey any regulations even when he does not agree with them, but only up to a point. Where that point is should remain a matter for his own independent judgment.

No doctor, or anyone else, should be so obedient that, on orders from a political or military authority, he would poison and kill humans for experimental purposes, as some German doctors did. No person should be so obedient that he will make his thinking conform to a pattern prescribed by any authority, civil, political or religious. At the most, only behavior should ever be obedient, never thinking. Without freedom of thinking, man is likely to be the lowest, rather than the highest, of animals.

We might well ask ourselves whether obedience in children is necessarily always a good thing. Suppose that a prejudiced white parent tells the child that he must not play with colored children. In this case it would be best for everyone if the child had developed enough discrimination to recognize the prejudice and lack of social development of the parent. He would surely be quite justified in continuing to play, even if secretly, with his friends, of whatever color their skin.

The obedient child tends to become either an obedient or a revolutionary adult. If obedience assumes a high moral value, the ability to think truly will have been crippled, and any refusal to obey will be emotional and violent, rather than, as it should be, calm and intellectually determined.

The too obedient child will tend to grow up with lack of confidence in his own thinking, and a need for direction by authority. He will be happy only when he is placed clearly in an order of superiority-inferiority, a sort of "pecking order" such as obtains in a flock of hens. He will tend to submit obsequiously to bullying by superiors, at least on the surface, though he may seek to sabotage the superior in the interests of his own advancement, and also to bully his inferiors.

He tends to be easy to convert from one authoritarian system to another. He may well look for and find new faiths to which he can sacrifice his reasoning power, and new representatives of those faiths whom he can adore and obey. In the field of ordinary living, the obedient child is likely to become a party hack, the obedient servant of a political machine, content to leave the thinking to a "boss" and to vote or smear or riot as he is told to do.

It may appear that training to be unquestioningly obedient is not desirable at all. What is really needed is self-discipline, which comes from identification with a parent who is mature, and from a reliable relationship with the realities of cause and effect, some early knowledge of human psychology and the ability to apply that knowledge to oneself.

The mature person is always under a sufficient degree of self-discipline, but only under the discipline of others by his own consent, for social purposes, or under rare, special circumstances. It is important that every adult be able to recognize circumstances in which he should, for social purposes or emergencies, submit himself to such discipline. If he is trained to unquestioning obedience in childhood, under the threat of loss of parental love and protection, he will not be able easily to develop that kind of discrimination.

Neither the regimented, that is, the obedient, nor the rebellious, who are still fighting against the demands of their own conscience that they obey, are what the world needs. It appears that obedience should not be a matter for conscience dictum at all, but for intellectual judgment. If that is true, small children should not be taught to obey, except under dangerous circumstances or emergencies or for social purposes in order to get along with the "local customs of the natives." When obedience is required by parents the reason should be made clear, even if the real reason is "I'm bigger than you are and can beat you into doing what I want you to do." That also may be a valuable lesson for the child; at least he is faced by reality and has to learn to live with it. "Mother knows best" is not always a valid reason; it is often applied when the question at issue is one about which Mother may be very ignorant or mistaken.

Of course such attitudes may make difficulties for parents; an obedient child requires far less thinking on the part of the parent than does a child who is learning to think for himself.

A child who has learned obedience of both thought and action has not learned to consider evidence. He is equally vulnerable to revelation, whatever its source or its medium. Mary Baker Eddy, Adam Smith, Mohammed, Hitler, Father Divine, the old Hebrew prophets, Gandhi, Christ or any of many others may equally well be accepted, depending upon the accident of birth, or particular emotional needs. Dr. Norwood Brigance, of Wabash College, in an address to the National Association of Teachers of Speech, said: ". . . every educated person ought to know when a thing is proved and when it is not proved, should know how to investigate and analyze the proposition that confronts him, and how to search for a solution, how to talk about it effectively before others, and how to contribute to a discussion on problems of joint interest." That kind of education is still very rare and it can become usual only as a result of much courageous thought and planning, but the ability of democracy to survive, and eventually to become valid for the world, depends on it becoming available for the peoples of the world. That will not be accomplished by people obedient to the rules of their ancestors or to the prejudices of their parents.

XV.

Development of Persons and Institutions

IN ALL cultures there has been a rapid development in the direction of technical training for most technical jobs. In the socially well-developed countries, positions in civil services are filled with qualified people and are protected from the political raiding which used to be so common.

In some countries a change in the party in power in the government still means loss of jobs for many people and employment for the friends and supports, or even, in the very backward countries, relatives of the successful politicians. These practices have been acceptable in every culture at some stage of development but, with increasing responsibility on the part of politicians, they are dying out.

The change seems to have come about, partly at least, as the result of the increasing complexity of the instruments with which people must work, and of governmental institutions, and the obvious necessity for trained persons to do the work efficiently, but probably more as the result of a gradually increasing degree of social responsibility among the politicians of most governments. There are exceptions in some places that are very surprising. For instance, in the United States of America, the very important position of coroner is still sometimes held by a person with none of the technical qualifications that are really necessary for that job, occasionally by a person without even a medical degree, and apparently for a reward for services to a political party or individual. No one seems to be able to explain this anachronism, except that irresponsible politicians like to have jobs with which to reward their supporters. That this situation is tolerated by the people themselves indicates one of the queer blind spots to be found in all cultures.

While in most countries such technical jobs are in the hands of qualified people, in political fields technical qualification, for highly technical jobs, is still rarely found or expected. There are still to be seen shocking cases where highly placed politicians, or even sometimes civil servants, are entrusted by their people with the responsibility of negotiating at international meetings of the highest importance without any of the technical qualifications such negotiation requires. Even yet there are to be seen national delegates discussing very delicate questions, in which are involved the prestige, the taboos, the special anxieties and hopes, and all the peculiarities of the peoples of many other nations, without themselves having had any appropriate preparation through education or experience.

Such responsibilities require, as minimum equipment, a knowledge of the religions of all the participants, the structure of their governments and something of their administrative methods, the major geography and the political divisions of their countries, their political parties and enough of their economy to know what is necessary for them and where compromises can be made, plus at least some knowledge of human psychology and minor psychopathology.

With even such a minimum of knowledge, no government could possibly press another country to do the impossible, as in the case mentioned earlier when Ceylon was urged, with threats, not to sell rubber to Hong Kong because from there it would go to Communist China. It is very shortsighted for any government to employ people who so lack understanding and foresight as to produce deep resentment and defiance uselessly.

People who would be horrified at the suggestion that they might trust their lives to an unqualified pilot of a transatlantic plane, or would not even employ an amateur to repair their television set, will elect completely unqualified people to positions of far greater importance, where their mistakes could cost the lives of millions of persons. The greatest responsibility of our legislative bodies, all over the world, is to ensure that our relations with other peoples in the world are friendly and co-operative, and do not become threatening to any of us, and yet we elect obvious neurotics, fanatically nationalistic or sectional in interest, or dominated by a particular religion, or just plain ignorant. We should not be surprised when some of them express even the ultimate and the most dangerous of all stupidities, in suggesting the possibility, or even the advisability, of a "preventive war." Only a few years ago such an irresponsible statement produced headlines all over Europe: "Senator _____ advocates not waiting five years but attacking Russians now." What should have been the feelings of horror and shame of the people who elected that senator!

The greatest danger in the world is that the Soviets might become convinced that they are going to be attacked very soon. It is not surprising that their delegates, and those from other eastern European countries, so frequently ask, "When do you think they are going to attack us?" It is never "if" but just "when," so effective have been the ravings of the said senator and others of his kind. When one tries to explain that no attack is intended, and that the senator is just talking to get the votes of fanatics in his own constituency, one is met by a stare of complete unbelief and the statement, "But that is impossible; no one would risk the lives of millions of people to get some votes for himself."

What would be the reaction in Western countries if highly placed statesmen in Communist countries were publicly to advocate immediate attack? The pressure to attack first would become overwhelming. Fortunately no one yet in eastern Europe has shown such irresponsibility.

Study should be made of what can be done about the attitudes of the kinds of people who elect irresponsible, untrained, even uneducated people to positions of great trust and responsibility. Clearly there is something wrong with those electors. They are not thinking truly in terms of cause and effect or they would see the danger to themselves and to their children in electing such misfits and such dangerous people.

Of course, the primary qualification for any position of trust where human relations are involved should be maturity, emotional, mental and social. Mature people do not lose their tempers and rant and rave. They are firmly related to reality and are not controlled by any authoritarian dogma or hierarchy. They can adjust themselves to changing circumstances and act for the welfare of all people everywhere, not just for those of some group, whether local or national. They do not harbor prejudices about race or color or ideologies, nor react to symbols as though they were real.

Only when there are enough such people in the right places can the nations begin to take a realistic attitude about the incompatible ambitions that divide the world now and threaten us all. There is no indication that any early mutually agreed solutions can be found for those incompatibilities. Only naïve wishful thinking could expect any real *rapprochement* at this stage of our development, that is to say, in this generation.

It is time we stopped getting ourselves all excited over friendly gestures designed only to ease a dangerous level of anxiety. The doctrine has not changed at all, on one side or the other, and the doctrines, in their present forms, are incompatible. At the same time we must recognize the fact that the old patterns of dealing with stalemates are now obsolete; warfare is in fact synonymous with suicide.

It follows that changes in one side or the other or both offer the only solution. The kinds of changes that are necessary will not be accomplished quickly on either side. Eventually the only real solution there can be will be something of the nature of a world federation or world government, in which all nations will invest some of their sovereignty.

The job of every country during the next forty or fifty years or so is to avoid war by whatever means are necessary, and to prepare themselves by education of their children to become part of a world community.

It is very doubtful whether national armaments can prevent war for as long as forty or fifty years; only a common police force can threaten and take police action without being a menace to nations. All military power in the hands of any one nation or combination of nations, short of a world community, is felt to be a menace by others, and will stimulate competitive arming. Perhaps soon some socially mature nation or nations will announce their willingness to supply armament and armed forces for control, and use as police, by the United Nations on a permanent basis.

If the nations are not yet ready to go that far, it may be necessary for us all to go on with the "cold war" for another generation unless, in the meantime, it might be possible for the United Nations itself, under the instructions of the nations in the General Assembly, to enlist and equip an armed force for such police action as the United Nations might need to initiate to maintain world peace. There would probably be no shortage of devoted volunteers for such a force, because of the hope for peace in the world it would bring.

While we are educating ourselves in that direction, we should also clear up all the discrimination between groups within our own countries, educate our children to be able to become world citizens, learn to control our own political and commercial aggression, and help all the people in the world who need help to raise their standard of living. That, of course, involves a drastic reduction in birth rates almost all over the world. Indeed, without that, all the rest would be useless, as the present rate of increase in population is negating almost all the current efforts in the direction of economic development.

Of course there will be long and perhaps violent resistance on the part of the immature, selfish, neurotic, the nationalistic, to the establishing of any kind of world government, for fear of losing some of the advantages now being enjoyed by a relatively few people, or losing some of their control over other people, which is always felt to be entirely for those other people's good. Perhaps the truest and most useful attitude mature people can take to this question of world government is that it is inevitable, that without it there can be no peaceful future for the human race or security for any nation or group, and that movement in that direction is our only sensible course. The inevitable vilification, smearing and abuse which will be used, in the absence of valid reasons which can be adduced against such a course, will gradually fade as more and more children are freed from dependence on authority and dogma, and freedom to think clearly becomes more common.

While the appropriate education of ourselves and our children for all these necessary changes is going on, there is much that can be done to improve our techniques of co-operation on a world basis. It is obviously unsound to continue to try to use many of our obsolete legislative and administrative methods and institutions for purposes for which they were not designed and which they do not fit. Practically all the legislative and administrative and political and business institutions of our countries have been developed for internal purposes. Wherever consideration of foreign relations has affected them, the purpose has been to gain advantage in some way, to acquire raw materials, sell surplus products, to encourage political support, or some such motive, but definitely not to improve the welfare of the foreigners or to help them with their problems. All our methods of doing business internationally have been designed and used as competitive weapons, to make money for our people, to enhance our prestige, to support political movements favorable to us; but now we, the nations of the world, have said in the constitutions of the United Nations and of its specialized agencies that we have signed, that we intend to co-operate for the benefit of other peoples equally with our own.

To do that effectively many of our methods must be changed. Many examples are available. For instance, the nations must find a way to provide reliable funding for at least several years at a time into the future for all their agencies. As it is now there are some countries whose legislative methods do not allow them to commit funds for more than one year at a time. Sometimes, because of legislative peculiarities, funds for the current year cannot be provided until halfway through that year or even later. On the other hand, in order to do their work efficiently, international projects have to be planned and preparatory work begun by the agencies with the countries concerned, often three or more years in advance. It has happened many times that an underdeveloped country has invested considerable amounts of money, time and energy in roads, buildings, training and supplies, over a period of two or three years of preparation, and then found that money for the project was not available. Such a situation is a heavy political liability within that country, and the blame is placed usually on the agency, where it does not belong.

It is really essential that governments make whatever changes in their legislative methods are necessary, so that they can provide financing at least three years in advance for technical assistance projects. Though some recent changes offer hope of progress, the present hand-to-mouth existence of the United Nations and the specialized agencies is most inefficient and inevitably leads to loss of confidence on the part of the underdeveloped countries in the good faith of the agencies and of the highly developed countries.

Until such arrangements can be made it would seem that the only sane way of carrying on the technical assistance programs is to earmark enough money out of the current year's budget to last for the life of each project, normally two, three or four years or sometimes more. This method would greatly reduce the amount of new work being taken on, but would ensure that each project would be carried on to completion, and not cut off because of varying amounts of funds being made available each year. To make that possible any arrangements whereby funds not expended at the end of the year go back into a common pot would have to be changed. Obviously budgeting for at least three years ahead would be preferable, but it may take some time for some nations to change their legislative arrangements to make that possible.

There are still a few countries which use such cumbersome administrative and legislative methods that they cannot take decisions, sign agreements or provide money at the rate required in a generation of telecommunications, airplane travel and rapid changes. It is essential for effective participation in world responsibility that every country which is still using nineteenth-century methods revise its administrative and legislative methods and institutions to make it possible for its representatives to negotiate, reach agreed solutions and sign those agreements without the necessity for delay or ratification. An administrative agreement without assurance of legislative agreement is worse than useless, as it only leads to distrust of motives and imputation of obscure intentions.

Where international agreement requires, as it does in some few countries of the world, administrative negotiation and agreement, then legislative ratification which may take one or two years or more, and then another legislative action to provide any necessary money to implement the agreement, the impression is given in other countries that such methods belong in the days of the sailing ship and camel caravan, rather than in the modern world. No country using such obsolete methods can carry its world responsibilities effectively, and they must be changed before it is possible to implement its intentions, no matter how co-operative and generous those intentions may be.

A further requirement of effective international co-operation is a degree of social responsibility among legislators that will ensure freedom of international policy, negotiation and agreements from the pressures of internal party or group politics within a country. There are few types of national behavior more destructive to good relationship with other nations than international maneuvers designed to obtain political advantage at home. There have been instances where some governments have avoided reaching agreements with other governments, holding up the whole world, in hope of reaping some party benefit in their own country. Naturally, and inevitably, the result is resentment and loss of confidence, particularly on the part of the friends and allies of that country. Its antagonists are always pleased at such evidences of insincerity or irresponsibility.

Stability of government is also essential to effective international co-operation, or at least continuity of policy and of personnel who negotiate and implement that policy internationally. Many countries, because of rapid and irresponsible changes of government or of personnel, have been almost useless in world affairs for months or even years at a time, and methods must be found by all governments which have not already adopted appropriate modern practices to provide the continuity in relation to other nations without which real co-operation is impossible.

There is only one country in which a national election almost completely paralyzes its international relationship for a year or more out of every four, the United States of America. The extreme and unique generosity of the people of the United States of America to other nations can hardly outweigh that exhibition of their scale of relative values.

These are only some illustrations of the many things the nations of the world need to do to begin to catch up in practice to their expressed intentions. Many of them need to be done at once, while the next generation is being educated to carry on from there to make a really peaceful world. Our major job, in every country, for this generation, is to revise our own ways of life in whatever directions are necessary to make it possible for us, and for more of our children, to function as responsible world citizens.

In all the cultures at which we have glanced, and in many others, are to be found individuals and groups who show relatively objective attitudes about their own countries, relative freedom from local prejudice and attachment to myth and dogma, and a relatively high degree of concern about world problems. Most of such people have been freed by their parents or have themselves grown beyond orthodox nationalism and dependence on the ancestral control. They are the people who have begun to do their own thinking and, though most of them are first- or at most second-generation freethinkers, they are doing an astonishingly good job of thinking appropriately to the new world in which we now live. Most of them are learning to identify themselves with the whole human race, not with just part of it.

Over much of the world, groups, often very small, meet more or less regularly to practice thinking clearly and free from parental, cultural and religious prejudice. Many such groups are anonymous, or just call themselves study groups; many are called Rationalists, Unitarians, Freethinkers, Humanists, and so on. Few of them are atheists in any absolute sense, but many are agnostics. They are all willing to change as circumstances change, and as they themselves learn more and develop toward emotional-mental-social maturity.

Most of them recognize, or begin to recognize, the desirability, and inevitability, of the establishment of some sort of world government. Attitudes about what that government should be like vary greatly, but discussions of that and other important matters tend to be amicable. They do not show the frantic impatience of the emotionally immature; their pressure for early action comes from a heightened awareness of the misery and fear in which many millions of fellow humans exist, and of the threat to the peace of the world and even to the existence of the race in the continuance of many of our present institutions and attitudes, and particularly of our narrow nationalism.

These people would seem to be "educated," according to a definition given by Dr. Earl C. Kelley (*Education for What Is Real,* New York, Harper & Brothers, 1947) : "An educated person would appear to be one who is able 'to relinquish what he has held, and build new habit patterns in keeping with new environmental demands.' " There are many new environmental demands with which our traditional habit patterns are indeed not in keeping, and there is a crying need for more of such educated people. Generally such people suffer only minor degrees of persecution from those who are faithful to the old certainties, but in some places—Spain, Italy, Portugal, Ireland, French Canada, some South American countries, some Moslem countries and a few other places on religious grounds; South and parts of East Africa and parts of the United States of America, the Belgian Congo and a few other places on racial grounds; Communist countries and a few other places on political or ideological grounds; India still, and in spite of determined attempts by the government to overcome it, on caste grounds—penalties for nonconformity may be serious. In all these places the independent thinker may suffer ostracism, persecution or loss of employment, and in some of them even death by government action, inspired mob action or lynching.

It is useful to remind ourselves that all peoples everywhere have gone through, or are now going through, or perhaps have still to go through, such stages of social childhood on the way toward maturity. Individual maturity, or at least growth in that direction, must precede social and political maturity. Increasingly it is apparent that individual maturity goes with freedom from the bonds of old certainties and loyalties, whether familial, religious, national or ideological.

Perhaps the most world-minded groups of people in the world are to be found in the secretariats of the United Nations and its specialized agencies. Many of those devoted international civil servants have developed to the point where they are capable of functioning as world citizens, not leaning toward special consideration for the welfare of people of any one nation or ideological or religious or other group. Also among some national delegations to international meetings are to be found a few really world-minded people, and in many countries there are some people at least who have grown beyond the narrow nationalism that is still standard for most of the world's people.

However, even among these leaders in the extension of social responsibility, there are still to be found many evidences of immaturity. In secretariats, delegations and practically everywhere else, jockeying for positions of prestige and influence, whether national or personal; emotional reactions, such as jealousy; inability to decentralize or allow others responsibility; sensitivity over loss of "face"; necessity to get attention and credit for oneself; "getting mad"; hurt feelings; antagonistic attitudes toward people with honestly opposed opinions; and many other such unreasonable and immature reactions are common. None of these evidences of minor psychopathology should have any place, or ever be seen in any meetings, certainly not among legislators or in meetings where nations are being represented, but they are still so usual that they are taken for granted as just "human nature."

Actually there is no evidence that such symptoms are necessary manifestations of human nature or anything more than the inevitable result of the distortions of human nature produced by our early training, which produces deep insecurity and anxiety, and of our competitive orientation. With a reasonable environment from infancy there is a reasonable hope that such inappropriate and destructive reactions could be reduced at least to the point where mature people could be elected to legislatures, appointed to civil services and sent as representatives of our peoples to meet with others of comparable emotional-mental-social development in international agencies. Of course, enough reasonable people at home to support those representatives' reasonable attitudes will still be essential.

XVI.

Education for World Citizenship

A DRAFT list of basic information which should be part of every-one's education, wherever he happens to be born, is suggested below. Much of this information is needed before school age and should be provided by parents. All of it should be made available to every person before the age of fifteen or sixteen, or whatever the term of compulsory education may be in the particular culture. Of course this is in addition to whatever may be necessary to live effectively in each culture. Reading, writing, arithmetic, geography, history, litera-ture, physics, a few principles of chemistry, a working language be-sides that in local use, physiology and public health principles, simple bookkeeping—all these and perhaps some others are necessary. Higher mathematics, algebra, geometry, trigonometry, organic chem-istry, Latin and Greek, and other subjects of specialist or of more advanced cultural concern might well be left for college. If children have some such background of information as suggested here, their learning at college level might well be much more efficient, less complicated by emotional upheavals and better oriented toward a planned future. If so, much more ground could be covered in college and some of the requirements now demanded for entrance to college could be waived.

WHAT EVERY CHILD NEEDS TO LEARN

I. *Reality*
   A. Time and space, the universe, the earth, present stage of knowledge and old theories taught at many times and places as faiths.

B. Life, evolution for millions of years before any "Creation" myths.
   1. Early forms of life, competing for survival and evolving in many directions. Many unable to compete and disappearing.
   2. Later forms of life, adjusting to changes or disappearing. Use of various methods of competitive survival, such as multiplication, size (very large and very small), armor (the shell, an external skeleton), teeth, claws, horns, poison, protective coloration, noxious odors, escape (swimming, running, climbing, flying), social organization (bee, ant), thinking, latest and most efficient, and developed in any high degree only in man.
   3. Latest forms of life.
      a. Domestic animals, changed by man by selective breeding for his own purposes. Also fruits, vegetables, grains changed to fit man's requirements.
   4. Biological reproduction, a more and more complicated process in an ascending evolutionary scale. Simplest cells, plants, amoeba, lower animals, vertebrates, fish, reptiles, birds, mammals, man.
   5. Mental-emotional life, how man's mind-body works. Brain and nervous system (functions not names). Instinctual urges to use all equipment. Behavior must be controlled for peaceful living together. Suppression and repression. A stable culture must provide socially sanctioned and sufficiently satisfactory direct or substitute outlets for all natural urges, sublimation. Imagination, its roles, free exploration, safety valve, allowing some outlet for socially unacceptable natural urges. Frustration, anxiety, temper, aggression, hostility, inferiority, displacement of affect (attachment of feelings to something to which they do not belong because not acceptable where they originate). Dreams, their roles, wish fulfillment, symbolic language of dreams.
   6. Conformity in behavior to agreed patterns necessary for group living, but only up to a point. Too rigid conformity destroys or prevents social development. The agreed patterns need to be changed with changing circumstances.

7. Freedom to think and imagine essential to man's survival and his social progress.
8. Obedience with discrimination, not automatic, self-discipline.
9. Myth and reality, the scientific method of knowing by observation, experiment and thinking, not by authority.

II. *Religions*
   A. Animism.
   B. Spiritism.
   C. Tribal gods, local gods in vast numbers.
   D. Movements and mixtures of gods and religions, adoption of one another's myths over centuries.
   E. The many savior gods.
   F. Death and resurrection of many gods.
   G. The one-god idea, probably developed in Persia.
   H. Major surviving religions, their origins, evolution and many conflicting sects, all depending on revelation.
      1. Hinduism.
      2. Buddhism.
      3. Shintoism.
      4. Christianity.
      5. Islam.
   I. Major religions or ethical or philosophical systems not depending on revelation.
      1. Confucianism.
      2. Unitarianism.
      3. Humanism.
   J. Agnosticism.
   K. Atheism.
   L. Rationalism.
   M. Marxism-Leninism.

III. *Social Development*
   A. Family, a patriarchic or matriarchic dictatorship.
   B. Tribe, a patriarchic, matriarchic or theocratic dictatorship.
   C. Principalities.
   D. Monarchies.
   E. City-states.
   F. Confederations.
   G. Empires.
   H. Communism.
   I. Democracies.

   } Great variations in all these.
   Most of them still exist and evolve slowly.
   All are experimental.
   No form is proven best for everyone.
   Further developments needed.

J.   League of Nations.
K.   United Nations and its specialized agencies.
L.   Regional organizations.

It would be relatively easy for any person who was introduced to all these facts in childhood to develop a firm hold on social reality, and relatively difficult for such a person to maintain a narrow and unchangeable religious, racial or nationalistic faith.

IV. *Economic Systems*
A.   Brief account of evolution of trade and commerce.
B.   Individualism and collectivism.
C.   Variations, conflicts and combinations, all experimental, none yet entirely successful in providing adequate distribution of goods and services to all people. Much further experiment and growth still necessary.

There will be no need to teach all these things in detail to children. The necessity is only to bring all these matters out of the field of taboo, where so many of them are now kept in most families and schools in most countries, and to do it early enough. All these, and many others, need to be kept in the "live files" in the minds of children and of adults; they all represent areas where the need for growth is urgent.

All the world's problems are in the minds of men and women, but they begin in the minds of children. There is no evidence that the barriers in people's minds to world co-operation and world peace are inborn, inherited or anything more than the inevitable result of the learning process to which almost all the world's children are subjected.

It should be possible, if we combine all our available knowledge and experience, to develop a method of education which will not produce these barriers to world co-operation and peace. It is conceivable that it might be possible to get sufficient agreement by enough people to have something constructive well under way within as little as two or three generations, or even less if we start at once. There are no other apparent solutions to the world's pressing problems which offer any promise within such a short length of time.

At first, of course, relatively few people will be prepared to participate in anything so foreign to our usual educational processes, but in fact there are some people, and a very few schools, now doing all they can in this direction, and co-operation from all such people can be counted on with confidence. There is much clear thinking available in this whole field, but almost all of it has been kept down, denied attention, ignored or challenged from the platform of old authority and dogma. It would appear that if the nations would learn how to live effectively, they must start freeing their children from the emotional-mental-social barriers from which almost everyone of this generation, and of all previous generations, has suffered. We are not free enough to do the job that needs to be done ourselves; we are too much tied to our loyalties of patriotism, religion and personal prosperity; but perhaps we can free enough of our children to enable them to develop to a stage of maturity appropriate to this changed world, though far beyond our ability to attain.

Of course there are risks in casting adrift from our traditional anchors of myth and dogma. Some of the newly freed people, unused yet to freedom and responsibility, may follow strange gods in directions that offer no real hope. Some may try to resurrect old dead gods in an attempt to back away from personal responsibility, and some, out of their fear of being different from the herd, may demand rigid discipline and conformity, with secret police, and witch hunting, and stool pigeons, and all the hangers-on of orthodoxy. But all those vain methods have their adherents now, and there is no likelihood that freedom to think will increase their numbers. Some of the newly free, and perhaps enough, may dare to proclaim, and live, the brotherhood of man without coercion.